T0209235

DEVELOPING
LIFE-CHANGING
FAITH

THE SIMPLE HIDDEN BIBLICAL KEYS
THAT INSTANTLY CHANGE
YOUR FAITH AND YOUR LIFE

CAROLE HAYGOOD

WESTBOW
PRESS®
A DIVISION OF THOMAS NELSON
& ZONDERVAN

Scripture taken from the King James Version of the Bible

WestBow Press books may be ordered through booksellers or by contacting:

WestBow Press
A Division of Thomas Nelson & Zondervan
1663 Liberty Drive
Bloomington, IN 47403
www.westbowpress.com
1 (866) 928-1240

ISBN: 978-1-5127-9053-5 (sc)
ISBN: 978-1-5127-9051-1 (hc)
ISBN: 978-1-5127-9052-8 (e)

Library of Congress Control Number: 2017909352

Print information available on the last page.

WestBow Press rev. date: 01/03/2018

Dedicated to my children and grandchildren.
I love you always and in all ways.

A special thanks to TJ
for helping me finish what I could not do for myself,
and helping me through it all;
and special thanks to JE & VE, KY, LL & LL,
LP & AP, and BP for your love and help.
Also, thank you to my teacher. I heard and learned well.
God bless you all.

Thank you to my Savior for teaching me the
faith I never thought I could have.
I write this to honor you.

TABLE OF CONTENTS

INTRODUCTION TO DEVELOPING
LIFE-CHANGING FAITH

Why write another book about faith? Everything has already been said about faith, right? I guess it depends on how you experience your faith. Let me ask you, do you have the type of faith that you desire? Do you have a rich and satisfying relationship with your Father in heaven and Jesus? Do you receive regular warnings and messages from the Spirit? Have you experienced many miracles? Do you know what kinds of miracles you can ask for, and how to ask so that God is able to given them to you? Do you know how to get answers to your prayers every time you ask? Do you know why God does not give you your requested blessings? There is a reason. If you cannot answer "Yes" to all of these questions and would like to have them as part of your daily life, and many more, this book is for you.

The Bible says that in the last days, knowledge (spiritual knowledge, aka: faith) will dwindle. We see this happening now. Yet, Jesus said, "If ye had faith as a grain of mustard seed, ye might say unto this sycamine tree, Be thou plucked up by the root, and be thou planted in the sea; and *it should obey you*" (Luke 17:6 King James Version [KJV], italics added). Looking at this verse as a guide to determine your faith, how is your faith? How do you generally feel about faith? Do you fear faith because you have heard about people gaining great faith through immense tragedy or loss, thinking that you may suffer, too?

When I started my journey toward faith, I did not have a relationship with our Father in heaven and Jesus. I believed in them. I said my prayers. My parents taught me to pray, and we said daily meal and family prayers in the mornings and at night. I went to church each week, participating in the youth programs. I even graduated from the four-year religious program in high school. As an adult, I was active in my church and brought my children with me. While most of my life consisted of religious activities, I had not built a relationship with God or Jesus. I did not even know how to start. The truth was, I did not believe that I was worthy of a relationship with them. I believed many false beliefs and misconceptions about our Father in heaven, about Jesus, and about me that kept me from believing that I was worthy of any more faith other than the simple belief that they exist. I did not even know *that* was not faith. Yet, I deeply desired to know the mysteries of God and experience the type of faith that I read about in Bible stories, but my set of beliefs kept me bound to spiritual mediocrity, until I accidentally stumbled into faith, and it changed my life.

Developing Life-Changing Faith involved a seven-year spiritual journey that led me to understand faith. This journey started when I accidentally used faith to be healed of an infirmity that plagued me for many years. Questioning how this miracle happened in this age, I turned to my unused Bible to find my answer. As I read the story that spurred the miracle, I questioned how Jesus allowed me to experience it because I believed that I was not worthy of a miracle from God. As I continued to ponder and question, the Spirit began to correct my misconceptions, changing my beliefs about God and Jesus, me as a person, and my beliefs as a Christian. A year later, I spent a year being educated about faith, and the subsequent years using what I had learned, being tested on it, and growing and strengthening my understandings so that I truly understood it. During my education, the Spirit led me to important key understandings in the Bible, hidden in plain sight. As I followed each key point, I was prompted to find tools that strengthened my faith and helped me to experience wonderful blessings, even miracles, creating a guide for developing the kind of faith that changes lives.

As Christians, we desire to have great faith. We love to read Bible stories about those who had and used great faith—those who fought giants, those who survived furnaces and hungry lions, and those who were healed by Jesus' touch—but many have difficulty understanding how to develop or use it in their own lives. They search for some hidden wisdom that seems to be known to some but is elusive to others. We are instructed to develop faith, yet many have trouble receiving answers to their prayers consistently enough to understand it completely, all the while fearing what developing that kind of faith may require.

Then the inability to discover the perceived mysteries of developing faith may have created misconceptions or false beliefs regarding it; about your Father in heaven and Jesus; and even about you, personally. Unless these misconceptions are cleared and corrected, faith will dwindle. Yet once seen, verses in the Bible will immediately clear all misconceptions, and they will change your life and bless you with the abundance of heaven's miracles, as Malachi stated,

> "And prove me now herewith, saith the Lord of hosts,
> if I will not open you the windows of heaven, and pour
> you out a blessing that there shall not be room enough
> to receive it" (Malachi 3:10 KJV).

As we continue toward the End of Days, the Bible warns us that the Last Days will be treacherous. We are in the end of the last days right now. We see that faith is waning and evil is growing on the earth.

> "This know also, that in the last days perilous times
> shall come. For men shall be lovers of their own selves,
> covetous, boasters, proud, blasphemers, disobedient to
> parents, unthankful, unholy, Without natural affection,
> trucebreakers, false accusers, incontinent, fierce,
> despisers of those that are good, Traitors, heady, high-
> minded, lovers of pleasures more than lovers of God."
> (2 Timothy 3:1–4 KJV)

The Bible warns us that evil will prevail for a time. There will be tragedies and calamities. We see these things occurring now in the seemingly back-to-back weather phenomena, terrorism, random shootings, "wars and rumors of wars" reported in our national and world news. We see that people are as the verse prophesied, "traitors, heady, high-minded, lovers of pleasures more than lovers of God." We see negative attitudes turning toward Christians who will be persecuted for their beliefs about Jesus. These prophesied occurrences will affect us so much that God will speed up time (and is speeding up time now) or "there should be no flesh saved" (Matthew 24:22 KJV, see also Mark 13:20 KJV).

As we approach the End of Days, we need the kind of faith that produces protections and blessings for us and our families—the kind of faith that is illustrated in the Bible. We need to develop and use faith as an active power. The Bible tells us how to do this. It sets all of us on a path to succeed using our faith, in spite of our human failings. Once seen (for they are hidden in plain sight), instructions on faith are clear, brilliant, and simple—simple enough for all people to follow and use successfully.

God desires for us to develop life-changing faith, for he knows that a great and powerful faith serves to build strong people who resist the influences of evil and can show others how to develop a similar faith in their own lives. It is not only possible to develop life-changing faith but is within all of our grasps, for God would not make it possible for some of his children to make it back to him and not all. So, faith must be simple enough for all to develop. And it is.

I testify to you in Jesus' holy name that these things are true, and are found within the pages of the Holy Bible. If you read, pray about, and practice the things in this book, as supplemental reading to your Bible, you will gain the knowledge and understanding to develop life-changing faith for yourself, and have the understanding and ability to successfully use your faith in your daily life, without fear or suffering. I know that God will lead you to the same knowledge and understanding that he led me.

A NOTE REGARDING THE VIEWS OF VARIOUS CHRISTIAN DENOMINATIONS

This book is intended to address biblical understandings of developing and using faith that will change your life. It is not intended to argue various theologies of Christian denominations. In my mind, different people need different ways to come to Jesus, and all Christian churches offer those different understandings. I have written this book with no intent to address any specific religion, church, or doctrine, but to write it in a way that you may put these concepts, tools really, into your life so that you may develop life-changing faith for yourself. The things that may be considered theological principles are my own understandings and beliefs that were safer than the beliefs that I had in my misconceptions. I wrote this book to share the tools that I received that changed my life and my faith. Even though my understandings may differ from yours, pray about the things that pertain to you and your spiritual journey, and leave the rest behind. It is all about what God wants for you, and learning things that may be beneficial to strengthening your personal faith and your relationship with Jesus. If you find things that are enlightening, great. If not, fine. The goal here is not intended to convert anyone to anything, but to gain powerful tools to enhance your faith in Jesus Christ. It is all about Jesus.

"Finally, whatsoever things are true, whatsoever things are honest, whatsoever things are just, whatsoever things are pure, whatsoever things are lovely, whatsoever things are of good report; if there be any virtue, and if there be any praise, think on these things. Those things, which ye have both learned, and received, and heard, and seen…, do; and the God of peace shall be with you." (Philippians 4:8-9 KJV)

1

BELIEF IS A CHOICE

> "For what if some did not believe? shall their unbelief
> make the faith of God without effect?"
> (Romans 3:3 KJV)

I congratulate you for choosing to start your journey developing life-changing faith. You will find that this journey is very exciting and far simpler than you will expect. I found it thrilling and very interesting. To start, we will need to do some housecleaning. There may be some misconceptions that may be lurking in the corners of your thoughts, beliefs, and emotions that may cause issues with faith. It is essential to identify and address them because misconceptions and false beliefs may take you away from Jesus, and prevent the development of faith. You need to be able to see what your misconceptions may hide and how to change them. Then, you will learn how your emotions may separate you from your Father in heaven and Savior. A genuine and honest relationship with them is essential to create this type of faith.

As we address each misconception, I will show you verses in the Bible that easily corrects them and leads you toward developing life-changing faith, showing you the same keys and understandings that the Spirit showed me. These biblical keys will immediately expand your understanding and your faith. Then, I will give you tools and show you how to use them so that you can successfully gain the results you desire. Because God is a god of order, we must learn how to do things in a way that he can answer (you need to do things the right way). I ask that the Spirit be with you as you take this journey, testifying of its truth. Let's begin developing life-changing faith!

Belief is the foundation of faith. Like a foundation strengthens or weakens a house, belief either strengthens or weakens faith based on the substance of the belief. To understand faith, you must first look at your beliefs. Some may hold misguided or false beliefs that may weaken or prevent you from developing faith. These misconceptions and false beliefs may be buried deep into your subconscious mind, or you may know them. Regardless of whether you are aware of your beliefs or not, you are guided by them. You need to address some of the main misconceptions that may prevent faith. Once they are cleared and the truth is restored, life-changing faith is simple and easy to create.

From before our births, in our mothers' wombs, we had the ability to perceive our surroundings. We heard and felt things that we did not understand. We created perceptions about the world, about ourselves, and about the people around us, and we carried them with us into this life. The more we experienced something, the more we began to believe what we perceived was true.

After we were born, other people added to our perceptions. Others' perceptions influenced our beliefs, experiences, perceptions, understandings, emotions, attitudes, words, prejudices, biases, etc. We will call them *thoughts*, for readability. We were influenced by others' thoughts through intentional teachings, or simply hearing what they said and the feelings that we felt when we heard them. The more influence they had on us, the more weight they influenced our beliefs, whether true or false. Our thoughts may have layered on each other and skewed truth, creating false beliefs that may have warped our view of the world, our lives, us personally, or those around us.

The good news is that all beliefs are chosen. At some point, you have either chosen to accept your beliefs as truth or you have created them by talking yourself into believing, by your own or others' thoughts.

Before my children learned their multiplication tables, they would ask me what 5 × 3 was and I would tell them the answer was 15. They believed that 5 × 3 was 15, even if they could not remember it the next time they asked because I told them the answer. Then one day, I sat them down with some candies and showed them that five piles with three pieces in each (and three piles of five in each) added up to fifteen, explaining that they could work out all multiplication equations in this same manner. I proved to my children that 5 × 3 was indeed 15 because I had them add five groups of three candies and when they counted them, they got the answer fifteen. They did not need to believe that I had the right answer any longer because they had learned how to figure out the answer for themselves, and they believed that I told them the correct process to figure it out.

Although this is a very simple example, all beliefs are created in that same way. Someone says something (or we have a thought, feel an emotion, or perceive a situation or attitude) and we either choose to believe it, or a belief is not created. Yet, the more we think a thought or perceive similar situations in the same way, the more we begin to see that the thought *must* be true, whether it actually is true or not. At some point, our minds have to validate an idea in order to accept it, just as my children's minds needed to validate my teachings, in the example above.

Some may argue that belief can be achieved passively, but it is impossible. Children are the best proof that we actively choose to believe or disbelieve. Many beliefs created in childhood were created because an authority figure—a mother, father, teacher, preacher, or television personality—said something and the child accepted their words as truth. Any idea could have just as easily been dismissed, as believed. Based on their personalities, many children require proof before they will believe anything (to the great aggravation of their parents), while others accept all that is told to them (to their own detriment).

"Train up a child in the way he should go: and when he
is old, he will not depart from it." (Proverbs 22:6 KJV)

A single thought developed in a moment of anger or shock has the power to create a belief. Emotions have a powerful effect on the creation of belief. Emotions to a thought are like putting miracle fertilizer on seedlings. Almost immediately, the thought is turned into a powerful belief because strong emotions validate the thought, in our minds. When an emotion is experienced, our minds accept the thought as truth, whether it is true or not. How many of us have heard a woman in tears proclaim that "men are evil," or heard a man punching a locker yelling "women are no good"? I am sure that each of us can think of several things that we started believing simply because we were upset at the time.

When I was a child, I sang all the time. I constantly had a song in my mind. Several years after quitting piano lessons, I started playing again because I loved to make music. I remember one afternoon, when I thought I was alone in the house, I started playing the piano and singing. I did not hear someone come in but I was startled by an authority figure yelling at me to "stop that noise!" I stopped, not singing again unless I was singing in a choir to be drowned by other voices. I did not know that my voice was *noise* until that moment, and the shock of the word *noise* silenced my music.

A few years later, my high school choir teacher begged me to audition for the Madrigals (the top performing choir at my high school) for the last semester of my sophomore year, something unheard of as a sophomore. I thought the teacher had made a mistake, so I did not audition. When he begged me to audition again my junior year, I auditioned and made it, which was a high honor because only seniors were given a position, at the time, but I had to turn it down due to family obligations. My big rebellion was to audition and accept a place in the Madrigals my senior year, regardless of family obligations—it was my last chance. Even with all of this and other positive vocal experiences, I still heard the person's words in my thoughts, believing that my voice was noise, until my granddaughter was born.

Since the first time I sang to my tiny granddaughter, she looked at me as if I had created the most beautiful cavatina ever created. She looked mesmerized when I sang. When she cried, I would sing to her as I readied the things I needed to help her (a diaper, bottle, etc.) and no matter how tired, hungry, or uncomfortable she was, she would stop and watch and listen to me with the same expression of magic in her eyes, as I sang. The way she looked at me when I sang to her showed me that my voice was not noise. To her, it was magic.

The strong emotions (the shock, sadness, and embarrassment) of someone yelling that my music was noise was enough to create a powerful belief that influenced how I thought about me and my voice, and limited my choices. Even though everyone in my life (including the person who yelled at me, that day) told me that I had a beautiful voice, it was not enough to change this belief because of the strong emotions I felt. It took the strong love that I felt toward my infant granddaughter, and her expressions when I sang, to realize that the belief was a lie. The weight of *this* relationship was stronger than the other relationship with the authority figure.

Just like these two people influenced my belief about my singing abilities, other people can also bias our beliefs, positively or negatively. People dealing with stressful circumstances, for example, may appear out of control when viewed from the sidelines. They may do or say things that they did not mean, in their stress and frustration. Then, any comments heard by another person can bias our thoughts and put more weight to it. If the comment is at all negative, it can create the belief in us that the stressed person is a "bad" person because the shock of seeing them in that state stunned all rational thought, in us (we did not know what to think about it, at the time, and the other person essentially explained the situation in the way that they either thought or wanted you to believe). Their words created and validated a new belief in you because the other person said it, whether true or not, when you simply had not been able to think about the situation, on your own, or gain additional information when the occurrence was over.

Yet, taking the time to learn the truth, questioning what is real, or looking for possible alternatives, we may have seen that the stressed person may be overwhelmed to the point of breaking, or may have needed help getting out of an abusive situation (if someone biases our thoughts, especially an adult who is teaching a child that the other person is "bad," the stressed person is being abused. Yet, the stressed person would have not told their children about it because they may have tried to deal with adult matters themselves, being a "good" parent, albeit flawed). You see how easily we can create false beliefs because of our and others' emotions and words.

False beliefs are created in many different ways and have the potential to cause problems in our lives. Some of our false beliefs may be detrimental to our spiritual, mental, or emotional health, and need to be corrected to set us free from the binds that hold us. A therapist, a counselor, or a wise friend may help us to *unbelieve* some of our beliefs.

We choose our beliefs and then have to try to survive the consequences of them.

Because false beliefs were created by suspended thoughts from powerful emotions, sometimes we can clear it by simply questioning or offering a different thought—at least it may offer a healthier one. Questioning our beliefs, particularly those that cause us pain, may be all it takes to move them from firm belief back to the idea stage where they can be re-examined. Then we can decide if it is a valid belief or one that simply needs to be tossed out.

Regarding faith, we may have been taught correct principles, but may have chosen to believe false perceptions and teachings, instead of truth. We may also have perceptions about ourselves that are absolutely false and cause us a great deal of difficulty with the development of faith, and more importantly, with our relationship with our Father in heaven and Savior.

I had several false beliefs that needed correction. I had a terrific teacher who had a gift of seeing people's beliefs that caused them problems. He questioned the beliefs that required changing. I held deep beliefs that kept me bound to feelings of unworthiness of God's love because I was born a girl. Somehow, I chose to accept it, and many others, as truths.

My teacher taught me that any belief that distances me from God and Jesus is a lie and is evil, and that truth only holds beliefs that bring me closer to them, without fear. He also explained that beliefs that make me feel bad about who I am, keeps me away from our Father in heaven and Jesus because it does not allow me to be close to them, and causes me to fear them. He said that if I cannot come to them without fear, for whatever reason, I am in Satan's grasp and am listening to his lies, instead of truth.

I questioned the thought. Could this be true? Initially, the thought appeared too self-serving. While I understood that beliefs that took me further from my Father in heaven and Jesus were evil, it took me some time to realize that beliefs that would bring me closer to them would also make me feel good about me, as a person.

It took an experimental acceptance to take a look at changing my beliefs. I looked at my beliefs that I held onto for so long—for all of my life—to see if feeling good or bad about someone would take them further away from our Father in heaven and Savior. It made sense to me that changing beliefs that kept someone from being afraid to turn to them would be evil, but this thought could not pertain to *me* though, could it?

I thought about my own beliefs. I understood that my beliefs caused me a great deal of pain, but I had been taught that to openly accept and feel love from God was prideful, and that repressing feelings of worthiness was humility and was necessary to return to our Father in heaven. After a great deal of effort, I finally realized that my beliefs were evil teachings and false beliefs, and were probably taught to cause blind obedience and control by those who had believed the same things themselves. Then, I realized that most emotional and mental pain was filled with false beliefs, for the same reasons.

Changing beliefs can be difficult, especially if you have held onto them so tightly, or if you believe that changing those beliefs would cause you pain or loss. Change is one of the scariest things to do. Like me, many may think that changing their beliefs, especially those you believe are righteous and keep you humble, may make you a bad person, or worse, an evil one. Yet, staying stuck into false beliefs keeps you stuck in the pain without an escape or help.

Using what I was taught, I learned that I could use my teacher's words as a barometer between good and evil. You can also know whether your beliefs, especially those that cause you pain, are good or evil by using this spiritual barometer:

> *Anything that distances you from your Father in heaven and Savior is evil and is from Satan. Truth only holds beliefs that give you a desire to be close to them without fear. You can tell if anything is good or bad by questioning whether it brings you closer to them or takes you further away—for anything that is evil will not bring you closer to your Father in heaven and his Son, where anything that is good will not take you away from them.*

The whole intent of this life is to make the choices that bring us to develop faith in Jesus Christ, accept the gifts of the atonement on a very real and personal level, and learn to hear and obey the Father's voice. All that we do in this life either propels us closer to or further away from Jesus. This is key.

I realized that identifying beliefs that caused me pain and made me feel bad about me, as a person, was the simplest way to identify those beliefs that needed to be changed. I could see that they propelled me further away from my Father in heaven and Savior because I felt that I was not worthy of their love. I also realized that humiliation is not humility, and *anything* that takes you away from Jesus is a serious sin. Fear is the key to finding false beliefs. Those beliefs that cause you to fear, for whatever reason and in whatever form, must be examined and questioned because fear is evil and is Satan's favorite tool.

Take a look at your beliefs, particularly beliefs that make you feel bad about you and may have a negative effect on your relationship with our Father in heaven and Jesus. Beliefs that distance you from God and make you feel bad about yourself need to be changed. Changing beliefs may only require tweaking, or they may need to be the opposite from the beliefs that you currently hold. The opposite belief was best for many of my false beliefs.

The first thing you need to know about changing a belief is that you must end up with a thought that is believable. If the new thought is something that you are unable to believe, no matter how close to the truth it may be, you will not be able to talk yourself into accepting it, no matter how hard you try. Remember that you were convinced of its truth for a very long time, maybe for most of your life. It made sense to you, and you accepted it as having validated proof, in order to create the belief.

To do this, first put the current belief into words. Many times our beliefs have remained raw emotions that have yet to be formed into words. Without putting the belief into words, it is stuck in the emotion and you can never understand it or do anything about it. Try to find words that most closely express the feelings and belief. These words may be few, such as 'I am unlovable,' or may be many and more complex.

Putting these feelings into words may make you feel emotional because it may be the first time you have actually understood the deep meaning of what you believe. The shock of the feeling that you are unlovable, for example, may hurt more than you can express, or it may help you to see that the belief is ridiculous, so you can simply dismiss it (like 'God does not love me because I am a girl).

Feel the emotions that you feel from the words you have written. Allow the tears that they may cause. Usually it only takes a few minutes, and then the feelings will fizzle out. Know that they will not hurt you anymore but they will only be felt. Feel the full extent of the emotion, and breathe.

Asking you to feel emotions that you have resisted for so long sounds irrational, but feeling them breaks the bonds created by your resistance. It is difficult to feel the idea that you are unlovable, for example, but feeling the emotions associated with the belief helps you to see the meaning that you have assigned to it. Only when you understand the meaning you have assigned to the emotions can you change or disprove the belief. Essentially, feeling the emotions soften the bonds, changing the belief from rigid concrete to something that is softer and more pliable, so you can let go of them quickly. Then the emotions can be tamed so that they no longer hold you hostage, leaving you with only the idea of the belief and the initial sting, which you can change.

Next, you must isolate what exactly it is that makes the belief so painful—again put this into words (e.g., "he wanted to hurt me" or "she hates me," adding the person's name or title, if possible). Many times, especially with beliefs that we formed as children, we tend to believe that another person wanted to cause us pain. It is the belief that another person actively desired to hurt us that makes it hurt now. The emotion of our belief is so raw that we feel threatened by that person currently, not realizing that the feelings happened a long time ago. Emotion does not understand time. With the passing of time, the unfelt raw emotion continues to change, expand, and twist because we have not laid it to rest or have not accepted the possibility of any other version of our viewed (or taught) events. Over time, our memories mutate, adding dynamic details that did not or could not happen, not understanding the truth in the events. We believe the absolute worst thought (or teaching) and accept it as truth. We do not realize that the simplest thought is closer to the truth.

The truth is that humans are only capable of the simplest thoughts, if any at all, when stressed. This is why your version and the other person's version are light years apart. Neither version is true. Both people were stressed and so neither was thinking, at that moment. You were both simply reacting to the shock. Then, if another person offered their opinion about the event, even if they had the purest of intentions, your thoughts were tainted by the other person's opinion, taking you even further from the truth.

If the pain was developed in childhood, without the years of experience to understand it (children are only capable of identifying with themselves, when young), it can also warp the thought of *you*, as a person, so much that you began to believe that *you* were bad or unlovable; or may cause general beliefs, believing that *all* in that category of people are bad. So, it is important to identify exactly what caused the pain in the belief—your meaning behind it. Please know that this is not truth. It is only the meaning that you have assigned to what you experienced, not really feeling or understanding any of it.

Take the words you used to identify its meaning and flip it around to words that mean completely opposite from the current belief and ones that do not cause pain (e.g., change "he wanted to hurt me" to "he loved me and wanted to please me"; change "she hates me" to "she loves me."). Notice that the first example required a secondary opposite thought—"he loved me…and wanted to please me." Make sure that you think about the emotions as you create the opposite belief to make sure that it is complete. Sometimes when we flip the belief, the feeling requires extra information to flip it completely. I am not asking you to believe this. This would be unbelievable because you accepted validated proof to believe the original belief, but this opposite thought is a good starting point. By flipping it in this way, you simply neutralize the emotions so that you can create a safer belief, using your mind and gut instincts, without the panic and pain caused by the original one.

Now, twist this new thought, keeping it in line with the thought that is opposite of the original belief, but moving it toward something that is believable and alleviates the pain. The easiest way to do this is to add as many negative and judgmental adjectives as you need to make it possible to believe, while ensuring that it alleviates your pain (try it. It does not end being judgmental or negative, and rids you of the negative emotions stuck in your pain). Some of the adjectives that you may choose, although you may use others not listed here, are *sick, twisted, crazy, mad, wacky, foolish, silly, insane, asinine, harebrained, scattered, unbalanced, unintelligent, thick, dull, brainless, dense, dim-witted, insensible, idiotic, stupid, warped, distorted, cruel, abnormal, disturbed, unhinged, deranged, unstable, uneven, bent, selfish, self-centered,* and then add a couple of extras, for good measure. Keep adding, changing, or subtracting adjectives and wording of the opposite of your belief until you come up with something that relieves your pain and may be possible to believe (e.g., "in his sick, twisted, evil, warped, distorted, stupid, selfish, dim-witted, idiotic mind, he wanted to please me and stupidly believed that he would not hurt me," or "in her selfish, self-absorbed, asinine, narcissistic, unbalanced mind, she loved me as much as she was able to").

Continue to whittle at and twist the new belief until it (1) no longer causes you pain. Once the statement has been devised effectively, you will automatically be released from the pain; (2) shows that the original belief can be a lie in some real and legitimate way. The statement should help you to see that the new thought is a real *possibility*, regardless of whether it coincides with your original belief or not. Instead, see if the other person's behavior may coincide with what you remember seeing and feeling, in the original occurrence, regardless of whether it is truth or not. The purpose here is to make a statement that *could be possible*; (3) puts the responsibility on the shoulders of the person to whom it belongs, if applicable. Know that a young child (0 to 9) cannot be responsible, and a child at any age cannot be responsible if the other person is an adult; (4) softens all bad feelings. All strong negative emotions keep us trapped in the emotions, keeping us from being all that we can be. Ensure that bad feelings about you are removed and that negative feelings about the other person have softened, if not removed completely; instead, feeling compassion or pity toward the other person, in their state; and (5) most importantly, that it allows you to be close to your Father in heaven and Savior without shame or fear. You may not realize this until the belief is accepted completely. In the beginning, simply ensure that there is nothing that keeps you away from them, like fear or shame.

I want you to clearly understand that this new belief will never be validated. The power of changing your belief in this way is that it holds the new belief as a *possibility*, where your old belief was rigid and concrete. It accepts that there may be other reasons for the other person's actions other than those you believed, and probably have nothing to do with you, at all. If you can see that the new belief is possible enough so that you can view the entire incident differently, you are free and can let go of the old belief that caused you so much pain. If you see that there may be another possible explanation why the other person treated you as they did, rather than believing only the overly dramatized version that caused you the most pain, there may be yet others. This realization shatters your bonds and your pain because you understand that you could not have seen things from their perspective, feel as they felt, and did not experience their pressures as they did, not being in their shoes. This means that you could not have had enough information to create a belief about them; their character, who they really are, their purpose, or their motives; or you can simply disregard it as something that happened, is over with and gone, which is something that you had not been able to accept before.

Now that your emotions have been addressed, investigate, in your mind, to see if you find other voices that are not your own or the other person's, in the incident. Did the person who hurt you all those years ago have a voice of their own, or do you mainly hear a third (or more) person's voice (perhaps an authority figure or someone else)? Were you able to hear or accept the person who hurt you when they talked to you, apologized, or explained, etc., about the incident; or do you only remember the third person's voice, *their* opinion, instructions, views, etc., and heard and accepted *that* person's words?

There are many types of abuses in the world. Most beliefs that hold the most pain also have an element of secrecy from a hidden abuser who also abused the other person but made them look like the 'good guy,' in your eyes. That third person may have made you believe that other person was a "bad" person. You will never be able to be free from your false beliefs while the secrecy is still intact, because you are perpetuating the secrecy and thus the abuse, as an adult. If the other person was manipulated in any way (meaning that a third party instilled in you the belief about the person, telling you that she/he was a "bad" person, and taught you to treat them disrespectfully), they need to be freed from their bonds, too. Secrecy is the clue that all that you believed was not true. They abused you by manipulating your beliefs to conform to that which they wanted you to believe, and treat the other person in a specific manner, for their own purposes.

Changing your old belief into its opposite (adding all of the negative adjectives) helps you to see that the other person may not have had sound judgment at the time of the occurrence. If they were acting as you described, in your list of negative adjectives, they could not have been in their right mind, for sure. If they did not have sound judgment, they may not be the evil person you believed them to be.

Look again to see the possibilities of underlying circumstances that they found impossible, acting that way, which you may not have seen or known about as you created your belief. If another person taught you that the other person is a "bad" person, for example, you would have treated them with disregard, disrespect, distain, etc., and *that* would have added to their pressures, not understanding why. If you were taught not to obey them and you should have, them being a person of authority over you, the added stress and frustration from your taught behavior may have caused, or added to, that person's behavior, even though you were innocent. You would not have appreciated the good things, the good times, or even gifts given. Everything you did and said would have significantly added to their stress, frustration, even anger, because of how you treated them, and your view of that person was tainted by the other person's control and manipulation. That impossibility made them react, rather than to act with a clear mind and choice, because of their inability to make things better, no matter how they tried.

This is the power of changing beliefs about other people in this way. Just because you would not act in the way they did (in your sound judgment) does not mean that they acted with sound judgment (in their stress), which your rigid original belief believed. Understanding that they reacted with flawed reasoning softens the hardness of your belief, and allows mercy, and possibly forgiveness.

General beliefs need to be handled a little differently and can be a little easier to clear. General beliefs are foundational beliefs about a category of people (i.e., gender, race, nationality) or may be a subset of people (e.g., blondes, overweight, nerds, etc.) or may be about you specifically. Those beliefs usually start with "all…," "they always…," or "I am…." (e.g., "all men/women are evil" or "I am unlovable"). General beliefs are thoughts that are exaggerated and amplified to the furthest end of possible belief and turned firm. It is a belief that all (or you) are that way. It does not allow for anyone to prove that it is not true, in your mind, which taints all future experiences because your mind seeks and only accepts additional examples showing you that you are that way.

To clear general beliefs, intentionally find ways that you see, in your own life, that the belief is a lie, and accept it. You may not be able to find any proof with the exact person, but you can find someone that proves that the belief is not true about you. "Women only want to hurt me," for example, may not be true about your Aunt Rose, your sister Kelly, and your childhood friend, Samantha, because you know that Aunt Rose, Kelly, and Samantha have always treated you well and would never want to hurt you. You have proven the belief is a lie because it is not true about *all* women. Another general belief would be the example, "I am unlovable." If your grandmother and your dog love you, you are not unlovable because your grandmother and your dog love you—they are able to love you and so you are lovable, to them. If you can find one person that does not fit with the belief, accept it. Your belief is a lie.

Choosing to accept something that you have believed for a long time may take some time to accept completely. Each time that you find a new example of the new belief, notice and add it to your mental checklist of examples, showing that it is true. This is what your subconscious mind did for you when you created the old belief. By intentionally noticing and adding new examples of your new belief to a mental checklist of examples, focusing on finding new examples, no matter how weak, you are intentionally proving and training your subconscious mind to notice the new examples, and forget the old ones.

Regardless of how you change your belief (use of the negative and judgmental adjectives or changing general beliefs with examples), you will know that you have constructed your new belief appropriately because you will feel a settling inside and the pain will dissipate. You will feel that a different light has been shed on the belief and you will experience a sense of contentedness. You will be free from the false belief forever because you have invalidated it, have proven that you did not have enough information to form a belief, and your mind (or you choose) accepts it.

If the belief that causes problems has to do with theology, however, it is easy to find verses in the Bible that either correct the belief or will prove that the truth is different from what you believed (like the belief that I am unworthy of God's love because I was born a girl, seeing that God created man and women, and saw that they were "good"). Also, pray for help finding the truth, and then accept it as truth. Once you have changed your false beliefs to safer ones, ones that alleviate pain and anguish, allow you to like, or even love, yourself, and allow you to be close to your Father in heaven and Savior without fear, your mind will support your new beliefs by validating the new ones because you now see and have accepted that the new thoughts are possible. That is how your mind works.

When you have intentionally chosen to change how you believe, your mind will learn to think in that way, judging circumstances and situations with understanding and compassion. You will realize that people (you and other people) do not always have perfect judgment, not being perfect, hoping that you receive similar understanding when you hurt someone else. Instead, they only knew what they knew and were able to handle as much as they did, at that time. This gives opportunities to watch the person from fresh eyes, without the tainted view of bias, focusing to see them differently. You will see for yourself that he/she is not as you believed. The information from seeing that we are all human helps you to let go of the painful memories and forgive (this is why adding negative and judgmental adjectives ends up not being negative or judgmental).

Are you causing some more false beliefs by doing this? Perhaps. We can talk ourselves into believing just about anything. Taking a belief that caused so much pain and changing it to one that you can live with, particularly if it is one that helps you to move closer to the Savior and feel his love, is a healthier belief regardless of its truth. The old belief was not true either, and you may never find the truth. The other person may not even know why they did what they did (or cannot say it, for whatever reason), and we need to forgive the other person so that we may be forgiven from the mistakes that we have done to another. It does not necessarily matter what the belief is, if it keeps you from being close to God, it is best to find a way to disagree with it so that you are able to have a relationship with him.

Our beliefs should allow us to feel our Savior's love without fear. He is the only being who can save us from the sins that would otherwise keep us from our Father in heaven, in this life and in the life to come. Changing our beliefs to those that help us to be close to them provides a good foundation on which to develop life-changing faith. We will all be corrected in the next life. None of us will be able to leave this life without the necessity of some corrections. Look at the beliefs that keep you distant from your Father in heaven and Jesus, and choose to make the changes necessary to bring you closer to them without fear.

2

THE WILL AND NATURE OF GOD

"Behold, what manner of love the Father hath bestowed upon us, that we should be called the sons of God."
(1 John 3:1 KJV)

Now that we have addressed our beliefs to ensure that none of them cause us to be distanced from our Father in heaven and Jesus, and understand about our emotions and the impact they have on our beliefs, we need to understand our Father in heaven and Jesus in order to build a relationship with them. I will use the general term, *God*, but it could apply to both our Father in heaven and Jesus equally. It is important to accept God's nature and his will, so that we work with him, and not against him. Many have misconceptions regarding God that get in the way of developing life-changing faith. Misconceptions about God cause great confusion and frustration as we pray to ask and receive blessings from him. Understanding his true nature helps us to know how to do things the way that God does, and builds confidence with him as we create a genuine relationship with him.

Some believe that God is an angry god who simply delights to punish, often in horrifying ways, or wipe an entire people from the planet. Reading parts of the Old Testament may give some that view, but it is obvious that they have not read it in its entirety. If they had read through the Old Testament, they would understand the true nature of God and what he wants for us. It is impossible to understand the type of relationship we can have with God with this belief.

There are many Bible verses that shed light on the nature of

God. Man, however, has a tendency to either not believe them or misunderstand them. For whatever reason, we literally take scriptural verses that show the wrath and power of God, but do not believe those that show his mercy and love. We choose to place a laser focus on his justice, but place a soft focus on his mercy; accept his wrath but not his love. By limiting our view to what we perceive as the "bad" side of God, not seeing his true and infinite nature, we develop beliefs that have warped God into a narcissistic, tyrannical, ultra-moody super-human, rather than the perfect God of light, truth, love, patience, and mercy that he is.

Many times we read stories in the Old Testament and see God's wrath. We do not notice that he was very merciful. We only see the devastations. We overlook the times when God listened and understood, allowing what the people wanted, blessing them, giving them more responsibility and position. One of my favorite examples of this was when the Israelites were near Jericho, when God wanted to divide the land for an inheritance, by tribe. Manasseh, son of Joseph, had a great-grandson, Zelophehad, who had a son named Hepher who had no sons, having five daughters.

Hepher's father, Zelophehad, was a counsel leader of the tribe of Manasseh. Dathan, a counsel leader of the tribe of Ruben, got two hundred fifty tribe counsel leaders riled up against Moses. They accused Moses of being the one who had killed so many people, since taking Israel out of Egypt, saying that it was all for *his* purposes and not God's, blaspheming God. To show the tribal leaders that God was the one who commanded Moses to do all that he had done, and that it was God's power that chastised them and took lives who were rebellious, God caused the earth to open and swallow them up, because these two hundred fifty tribal leaders could lead all of Israel into a rebellion against God and God's appointed leader, Moses (Numbers 16:21-35 KJV). Hepher's father, Zelophehad, was among those who had been swallowed in the earth, leaving no male heir for an inheritance, even though Hepher was a righteous man.

So, the daughters of Hepher approached Moses and Eleazar, the priest, and asked if their father would receive an inheritance, having no sons. Moses inquired from God, and God told Moses that the daughters of Hepher were correct and that their father should receive an inheritance (Numbers 27:1-7 KJV). Because of this inquiry, an entire section of the Law was added, giving an inheritance to daughters, if there was no male heir, and what they would do with the land when they marry or if they had no children. There are many similar examples, in the Bible, like this one, showing God's care and love toward his children.

There are a few important things that we need to understand about Moses' writings. First, Moses wrote with very little detail. You could say that his writings were bullet point lists of occurrences. These are small snapshots of some of the more important happenings in the wilderness. Looking at the pages of your Bible, you see that Moses had relatively few pages, in his writings, to report the Law and the happenings during the forty years in the wilderness. That does not allow much detail. Second, reading the books of Moses (and from his own explanation [Exodus 4:10 KJV]), we see that he had few words, possibly having a speech pediment of some sort; and being more methodical or analytical in his personality, more concerned about doing things correctly, in God's eyes, than anything. Third, the Israelites did not know how to think or act on their own. The Israelites had been slaves, doing and thinking what their task masters told them to do, for generations.

While God started with small consequences to train them his ways, it is clear that they did not have the capability to understand how to act appropriately without large consequences, to teach them. They did not learn even when the basic commands were written on stone tablets—the Ten Commandments. They easily fell into doing things the way the Egyptians did. God wanted them to think differently—doing things his ways. He could not allow them to go to the Promised Land until all of the thoughts and actions of Egypt were cleansed from them. This is why they had to endure the hardships of the wilderness for forty years. They would have been able to go straight to the land that God had for them if they quickly understood and adopted his ways. It was the people who needed the large, devastating consequences, in order to soften their hearts and adopt his understandings, so that God could teach them.

In our own lives, if we quickly learn to understand our Father in heaven and Savior, learn to understand, and adopt his ways, the chastisements do not need to be large, devastating events. If we change ourselves to be more like Jesus, we will learn about him without learning the hard and painful lessons, too. This is key.

During all of the many chastisements, all of the times of rebellion and murmuring (whispers of discontent), not learning about what God wanted from them, he could not take them to the promised land until they did learn. He always softened and brought them the blessings that they needed, however, once they humbled themselves, always forgiving them and being faithful in blessing them. Then we see the Father's faithfulness as God led their armies to take the cities that God had commanded to take for his people. These people were not warriors. They had been slaves in Egypt. They should not have been able to take cities and peoples. We see how faithful God was toward his people.

Our Father in heaven and our Savior want to help and bless us so much more than we can comprehend. We see the Father's willingness to help in many Bible stories. We see it in the stories about the prophet, Elijah. God took care of Elijah throughout his life, providing for all that he needed. One time, he led Elijah to water during an especially harsh drought. He told him of a secret brook from which he could drink. Then he sent ravens to bring bread and meat for him to eat. When the brook dried up, he went back to God, who told him to go to Zarepath. He was aware of a widow who was in need and so orchestrated the meeting of Elijah and this woman, telling him to stay with her and she would feed him. When Elijah arrived, he found the woman gathering sticks for her and her son so that they could eat their last meal before they died, for she had only enough flour and oil for one last meal. Did God not know that she only had one meal of flour and oil? Of course he knew. It was for this purpose that he commanded Elijah to go and find her. He knew that the woman would give all that she had to a stranger (as she did not know that he was the prophet, at the time), and this act would provide the means to bless her.

Elijah told the woman to make the cake for him first, which she did. With this small test of faith, he commanded that the flour and oil continue until the rains came again. But it seems that they had been eating a meager amount, because the woman's son died. She laid her son into her bed and went back downstairs, feeling assured that he would not need to suffer, as they die. Elijah went up and prayed to God, and laid upon the still child, doing the same thing three times, until the child revived. Not only did God provide for Elijah, he also knew what was going to happen to the woman's son and so provided a way for him to save Elijah, the widow, and her son. (1 Kings 17 KJV)

We see God's patience and his willingness to listen to all of that we say, when Abraham questioned God about the destruction of Sodom and Gomorrah. Abraham questioned God if he would destroy the cities if there were fifty righteous people in the cities. God told Abraham that he would spare the cities if there were fifty righteous. But Abraham was still concerned and questioned God's righteousness when he asked, "Shall not the Judge of all the earth do right?" (Genesis 18:25 KJV), yet God was patient with Abraham because of his humility. God allowed him to question time and again, whittling down the number to forty-five, forty, thirty, twenty, and then to ten, each time patiently telling Abraham that he would not destroy the cities if that number of righteous souls was found, all the while knowing that there was no righteousness there (Genesis 18:20-33 KJV).

We also see the Father's mercy toward Sarah and Abraham, giving them a son in their old years. Throughout the entire Old Testament, we see the grace (kindness, favor, goodwill, etc.) of God. In all of the stories, we see that God leans toward mercy, pity even, toward his people.

From the beginning when God created the earth, he made everything very good. God did not ever create anything that was not very good. He always gave the very best. He created all things for our good, for our success, for our happiness, for our fulfillment. Looking at consequences and chastisements, we see that even they were for our good, to teach us the right and good ways to live, so that he is able to give us a blessed life and ensure that he can take them home, in the next life.

One of my favorite Bible stories is the story about Jesus' mother who was hosting a wedding party and ran out of wine (John 2:1-11 KJV). Knowing how important the wine was for the wedding party (and so that she was not viewed as a bad host), Jesus turned several jugs of water into very fine wine—it was not cheap wine or even wine that would have been acceptable, it was very fine wine.

Jesus turning water to wine had nothing to do with it being his mother for whom he performed this miracle, and more to do with her need and her faith. Remember, God is no "respecter of persons" (Acts 10:34 KJV) and Jesus did the will of his Father perfectly, so to do this for his mother, favoring her over others, would have caused him to err. He gave us the perfect example, so he did not err. Yet, look at the types of Mary's need. Her needs were emotional (to prevent her embarrassment) and temporal needs (to give a good wedding party and retain her standing in the community).

This story is so very important to understand the nature of our Father in heaven and his Son. More so than any others, this story helps us to understand that God is interested in every aspect of our lives—even our feelings. Everything that is important to us is also important to God. This means that our cars as well as our testimonies are equally important to God. Likewise, our jobs and our church service. Our lost keys and our Bible study. All things of this life are important to God because all things either add to or detract from our faith in Jesus. So, to be willing to bless us with all righteous desires, both temporal and spiritual, adds to our faith and testimony in Jesus, and therefore adds to his purpose and his joy.

> "Ask, and it shall be given you; seek, and ye shall find; knock, and it shall be opened unto you; for everyone that asketh receiveth; and he that seeketh findeth; and to him that knocketh it shall be opened. Or what man is there of you, whom if a son shall ask bread of any of you that is a father, will he give him a stone? Or if he ask a fish, will he for a fish give him a serpent?" (Matthew 7:7–10 KJV, see also Luke 11:9–13 KJV)

This is a question Jesus asked when teaching about how God gives to his children. Of course, we would not give our son a stone when he asked for bread or a serpent when he asks for a fish. We would not only give him what was asked, but would sit him down and make him bread and fish, and more. As a parent, if our child is hungry, we feed them amply, no matter their age. We would feed our child everything we have, if necessary, and then we would take him or her to the grocery store and fill up a shopping cart of groceries to fill their pantries. Then we top off their gas tanks, and our wallets would be opened, putting twenty, fifty, a hundred or more dollars into their shirt pockets, assuring them that the money given was not a loan that would require repayment. God not only gives what is given but makes sure that it is the very best, just as Jesus turned water to fine wine. It is not just what would be acceptable; it would be the very best of what was asked.

The story of the prodigal son illustrates this point, too (Luke 15:11–32 KJV). A father, when he saw that his son had returned home, slaughtered a fatted calf and had a celebration because he was so very relieved and happy to have his lost son back. Yet, looking at the son's predicament, when he decided to return to his father's house, he only wanted a roof over his head and food in his belly, wanting only to be a servant in his father's house. He understood that he had squandered his inheritance and so was not worthy of more, in his mind. He was overwhelmed when his father put on his best robe, a ring, and sandals, and celebrated his return home, not even asking about the money or why he had returned. He was simply happy and relieved that he was home. Just as we generously give to our child that which they ask, God generously gives to us that which we ask, too; and just as we celebrate our child's return, God celebrates us when we return to him. Jesus continued in Matthew 7:11: "If ye then, being evil, know how to give good gifts unto your children: how much more shall your Father, which is in heaven, give good things to them that ask him?"

All things of this life are spiritual, and God can give us spiritual things in temporal ways. God is very concerned about the food we eat, the clothes we wear, and whether we have a roof over our heads. God cares about our temporal lives just as much as he does our spiritual lives. Why else would Jesus tell a disciple to catch a fish and pull a gold coin from his mouth to pay their taxes (Matthew 17:27 KJV)? Jesus did not want them arrested for not paying their taxes.

The widow who went to the prophet, Elisha, and told him that the creditor was on his way to take her two sons to the bondsmen, would have been given a reward in heaven instead of miraculously filling as many vessels as they could find (even borrowed ones) with oil to sell, to pay her debt and keep her sons home, if temporal needs were not important to God (2 Kings 4:1–7 KJV).

Another is the story of the Israelites receiving manna from heaven (Exodus 16 KJV). The Israelites were starving in the wilderness. Moses prayed and God rained manna from heaven every day. Yet he not only gave them manna every day, he also brought quail, which he did not need to bring. Manna, being a seed, would have had enough nutrients to feed them well. Seeds have good amounts of proteins and vital nutrients sufficient to keep them alive. But God gave them more than just enough to keep them alive; he brought quail to them every evening. If God was not concerned about their satisfaction, he would have supplied enough manna to keep them alive, but not satisfy each individual's desires, or bring quail every evening for their supper, which would have been more than what was necessary. He also wanted them to be satisfied.

If you think about it, Jesus would not need to give the blind their sight or the lame the ability to walk if he was not interested in their lifestyles and standards of living. If God was not interested in our physical needs and wants, many of the healings would not have taken place because only the casting out of devils would be spiritually necessary.

Going back to the first story, Jesus would not have turned water to wine for his mother who was hosting a wedding party. This was not even for survival. This was to keep her from being embarrassed and spoken of as a bad host, and to ensure a good wedding party for the guests.

There would be no need to be instructed to pray over our flocks and crops and animals if not for temporal reasons. We do not need any of those for spiritual reasons—and since Jesus had come to fulfill the old covenant, he knew that soon the people would not need animals for sacrifice, being himself the last Lamb to be sacrificed. Furthermore, we would not be commanded to give to the poor if their temporal needs were not of any consequence to the Father. All things are important to God.

I learned this concept through my fear of beetles. I grew up the eldest child of two brothers and four sisters, in that order. There are six years between me and my closest sister and so I grew up with my brothers, who were pranksters. As children, we visited our grandparents in Idaho every summer. We loved to sleep out in their camping trailer. On more than one occasion, my brothers went out and gathered as many June bugs (aka, Ten-Lined June Beetle or Watermelon Beetle [Polyphylla decemlineata]) as they could find and put them in my sleeping bag, waiting for me to slip inside with them, not knowing that they were there. They would screech such a horrible sound, and their hooked legs would stick to my nightgown and I could not get them off of me. To this day, my nervous system goes haywire whenever I see a beetle—even a picture—and the thought of one being in my home is enough to keep me awake at night for weeks on end.

Because of my reaction of the thought of beetles in my home, I took my fear to my Father in heaven in prayer and asked him to protect my home from any type of beetle, especially bed bugs and cockroaches (thankfully, I have not had these problems but I cannot imagine what would happen, if I had). I did not know that God had protected my home from beetles until I received a chastisement from him in the form of a bed bug crawling across the bathroom floor, with a wordless message to my mind that told me "I can remove the protection...," letting me know clearly that I needed to obey. My first thought was that I did not know that he had protected my home, which was followed by the message, "You asked me to...."

From this simple yet powerful experience, I learned that God is interested in all aspects of our lives. It showed me that he was interested in my fears and phobias, which I usually discounted as unimportant. I was also surprised to learn that he granted the protection of beetles only because I was afraid of them. This is why the story about Jesus turning water to wine is so important. It shows us that God is interested in all parts of our lives, not only our spiritual lives. Since Jesus turned water into wine for Mary, it means that we can ask for emotional things too.

After learning about faith and understanding how God loves us and does not want us to fear, I have prayed for God to appease specific individuals. Dealing with difficult and demanding people, people who are overly judgmental, or those who have tried to harm me can be complicated and frightening. Thinking about Mary's potential embarrassment, I realized that it may be a good idea to try asking God to appease them, and God pacified each one and made them easier to deal with.

Our Father in heaven is concerned about things we deal with daily, especially things that cause us to fear or make us uncomfortable. God allows us to experiment with all aspects of our lives to see what we can learn about him and his Son. Asking our Father in heaven for blessings is one of them. Experimenting by asking him for things, help, protections, appeasement…, all sorts of things, we learn about him. The worst thing that he will do is to tell you "no," but Jesus did not refuse anyone, so he will not refuse us either.

Foundationally, God's nature is about order, equity, and love. Order means that everything has a place, time, and way. Equity is part of order. Equity is more than equality. It means that all is fair, just, and equal. Love is a principle of equity, as is order. Understanding that love is a principle of equity and order, we glimpse the true and eternal nature of the High God. With God, there is no favoritism: what he is willing to do for one, he is willing to do for all. That being said, we can place ourselves in a place of favor with the Father, equitably.

Equity does not mean that all people are given all blessings and favors regardless of their choices and obedience. That type of equality would not be fair or just. Instead, our Father in heaven offers blessings and favors to all and allows us to choose whether or not to do what is necessary to obtain them. This is equitable and fair and just.

While we are unable to comprehend the extent of our Father's qualities, he not only possesses them, but is filled with them—100%. All things are done through his great love toward each of us, including chastisements. Our Father in heaven wants us all to choose to return to him. He made it possible for all of us to return to him by making the requirements simple enough so that all are able to successfully accomplish them. He would never take away that choice and make it for anyone, because the choice itself is too important. God knows exactly what is awaiting us should we make the choices to accomplish the requirements, and he is willing to do whatever is necessary to ensure that all those who desire to return to him can do so—it is that simple. He is willing to discipline us, chastise us, remove blessings and protections, give promptings, teach us, give us miracles, bless us, etc., to set us straight on the path toward Christ and let us know when we have moved in the wrong direction, from his perfect perspective.

God's justice is true justice. He righteously judges and reproves as a parent corrects a child, teaching rather than punishing. God does not punish. Instead, he removes his protection and leaves us to our own devices, allowing the natural consequences and our own choices to correct us. While he has the power to slay the wicked, he is more about correcting his children and allowing us to see his ways, always pouring upon feelings of love and patience, when he corrects. Jeremiah states it well:

> "Thine own wickedness shall correct thee, and thy backslidings shall reprove thee: know therefore and see that it is an evil thing and bitter, that thou hast forsaken the Lord thy God," (Jeremiah 2:19 KJV)

People get hung up on the wording of Isaiah:

> "But with righteousness shall he judge the poor, and reprove with equity for the meek of the earth: and he shall smite the earth with the rod of his mouth, and with the breath of his lips shall he slay the wicked." (Isaiah 11:4 KJV)

Here, Isaiah shows the power and equity of God. Many times we think that this verse shows God's level of love and mercy as being small or nonexistent, but we would be mistaken. There are two sides to this verse. With his righteous judgment, God does judge the poor and the meek. The poor and the meek are those who are not only financially poor but those who have been humbled by life's circumstances through disease, ailment, disability, betrayal, manipulation, or otherwise experienced difficulties. The poor could also be those who mourn or are poor in spirit. The meek are those who are soft-spoken, humble, and mild-mannered. On this side of the verse, it shows God's mercy and love because he is not the high-and-mighty judge that we think. He would mostly judge with a soft hand, as he judges the poor and meek, with absolute equity, allowing for their inabilities and experiences. All the same, he reproves, chastises, and corrects, bringing people who stubbornly cling to their false beliefs into a position whereby they are humbled and can be lovingly corrected, at what level the individual requires, based on their willingness or ability to listen and obey him. On the other side of this verse, with his word he can slay, destroy, devastate, or defeat those who stubbornly and rebelliously choose to remain in their wicked and evil ways. Isaiah illustrated both of God's abilities: his mercy and his power. These are two separate ends of the spectrum. Our Father in heaven can do all, based on our capacity and choices. This verse illustrates God's equity perfectly.

To understand the true nature of God, it is best to simply view him as a perfect, loving, and merciful Father who has the power and ability to do all things but prefers not to use his might unless necessary. Know that we will not be able to understand the infinite nature of his equity and justice, in this imperfect life, but because of the atonement, God is able to extend his great mercy to us, where he could not do so before due to the necessity of perfect justice.

In the beginning of time, we see that he extended great mercies toward man:

> "Know therefore that the Lord thy God, he is God, the faithful God, which keepeth covenant and mercy with them that love him and keep his commandments to a thousand generations;" (Deuteronomy 7:9 KJV)

This is the promise of the Good Shepherd recorded in Moses' day. The Good Shepherd promised to save the descendants of those who were faithful. The faithfulness of those who love him and keep his commandments ensures their children's salvation to a thousand generations. He finds them and brings them back into the fold for a thousand generations (the term "a thousand generations" does not mean a literal number, according to Hebrew text; rather it means all of their descendents for all time. Since we have had less than two hundred generations since Adam and Eve currently, we would have more than

eight hundred generations to go [yet we are at the end of the Last Days].
That is an amazing amount of mercy).

Throughout the Bible we see the love and mercy of God. Here is
another one:

> "I the Lord thy God am a jealous God, visiting the
> iniquity of the fathers upon the children unto the
> third and fourth generation of them that hate me, and
> shewing mercy unto thousands of that that love me and
> keep my commandments. O that there were such an
> heart in them, that they would fear me, and keep all
> my commandments all ways, that it might be well with
> them, and with their children for ever!" (Deuteronomy
> 5:9–10, 29 KJV)

Combine the last verses with the verse we discussed earlier. God is
merciful and remembers the covenant of those who love him to a
thousand generations that it might be well with them and with their
children forever; but only visits iniquity upon the children of those who
hate him to the third and fourth generation.

> "But the mercy of the Lord is from everlasting
> to everlasting upon them that fear him, and his
> righteousness unto children's children; to such as
> keep his covenant, and to those that remember his
> commandments to do them." (Psalms 103:17–18 KJV)

> "For we ourselves also were sometimes foolish,
> disobedient, deceived, serving divers lusts and pleasures,
> living in malice and envy, hateful, and hating one
> another. But after that the kindness and love of God
> our Savior toward man appeared. Not by works of
> righteousness which we have done, but according to
> his mercy he saved us, but the washing of regeneration,
> and renewing of the Holy Ghost; which he shed on

us abundantly through Jesus Christ our Savior" (Titus 3:3–6 KJV, see also Micah 7:18–19 KJV).

God gave us commandments that would place us in a position to get through this life with as few bumps and bruises as possible. We are foolish children, sometimes needing to learn hard lessons the hard way. Yet, he disciplines us to guide us through the narrow and straight gate that leads to our greatest joy: being with our Father and our Savior again. In this, we see the true nature of God. To ensure that we all have the ability to return with him again, our Father chastises and disciplines us through arms of order, equity, mercy, and love.

> "For a small moment have I forsaken thee; but with great mercies will I gather thee. In a little wrath I hid my face from thee for a moment; but with everlasting kindness will I have mercy on thee, saith the Lord thy Redeemer... For the mountains shall depart, and the hills be removed; but my kindness shall not depart from thee, neither shall the covenant of my peace be removed, saith the Lord that hath mercy on thee. O thou afflicted, tossed with tempest, and not comforted, behold, I will lay thy stones with fair colours, and lay thy foundations with sapphires. And I will make thy windows of agates, and thy gates of carbuncles, and all thy borders of pleasant stones. And all thy children shall be taught of the Lord; and great shall be the peace of thy children." (Isaiah 54:7–13 KJV)

A story that my late husband told me, just before he died, reinforced God's love toward all of his children. He was several years older than me. Looking back, I suspect that he sensed that he was ill, although he would receive a diagnosis a year later, because he begged God to bring someone into his life so that he did not die alone, being one of his greatest fears. This prayer spurred our meeting. When he proposed, I took my prayer to God, not wanting to make a painful mistake by marrying foolishly, which is one of my greatest fears. Because I had not yet recognize the Spirit then, I asked and received seven confirmations, the last one stronger than the others, telling me that this is an answer to his prayer and that God wanted me to do this, asking me to do so. So I did. He was diagnosed with advanced leukemia about a year later.

My late husband's fear was to die alone and so our Father in heaven found someone who he knew would be willing to do anything for Jesus (me), because of his greatest fear. He also knew that my greatest fear was to foolishly marry, and so he patiently answered my question seven times, all the while telling me the answer louder each time to ensure that I understood that it was an answer from God, because of my fear. When you add my fear of beetles onto the mix, we see the patience, mercy, love, and grace of our Father.

Our Father in heaven is so compassionate, so kind, so patient. Whatever we ask, if it is a righteous desire and we ask in a way that he is able to answer, he will do it for us. It is that simple. He recognizes our fears, our heartaches, and our longings. Because of his loving nature, he is willing to orchestrate things that will calm our fearful emotions and make us happy, if he sees that our hearts are his Son's and are trying to follow him. This is key.

The Bible verses regarding God's attributes and nature are literal. He truly loves and knows each of us with a love that we cannot fathom. Experiencing his love, which is most likely only a small portion of the love that he possesses, is overwhelming, it is so immense; but all the same, you wish that you could feel it always. Understanding that our Father in heaven is willing to bless us with anything that we want or need (which he is), or at least accepting it, takes some of the pressure of knowing what blessings we can ask for. Because asking and receiving teaches us much more about our Father in heaven and Jesus than we can learn in any other way, asking and receiving are necessary to developing life-changing faith. Understanding that God is so very aware of all aspects of our lives helps us to trust him enough to ask.

> "Are not five sparrows sold for two farthings, and not one of them is forgotten before God? But even the very hairs of your head are all numbered. Fear not therefore:

ye are of more value than many sparrows." (Luke 12:6–7
KJV, see also Matthew 10:29–31)

"For God so loved the world, that he gave his only
begotten Son, that whosoever believeth in him should
not perish, but have everlasting life. For God sent not
his Son into the world to condemn the world; but that
the world through him might be saved." (John 3:16–
17 KJV)

"For as the heaven is high above the earth, so great is his
mercy toward them that fear him." (Psalms 103:11 KJV)

Please know that the word *fear*, in the Bible, does not literally mean
to fear God, but to be humble and reverently revere him. Basically, it
means to worship him.

Accepting God's true nature and learning to obey him are not
difficult things, but they go far to gaining the type of relationship that
we may have with him. Knowing that he is filled with patience, mercy,
love, and other attributes, we can turn to him and be close to him
without fear. If you do not know it now, ask that you accept that it is a
possibility, so that you can test it. Once you try, the Father will show
you that it is true, and will teach you in his perfectly wonderful way.

3

OBEDIENCE AND FAVOR WITH GOD

"If ye love me, keep my commandments."
(John 14:15 KJV)

God is a being of great power and mercy. To view God as our Father who loves us and is willing to do all in his power to help us home, makes it easy to trust him and surrender our will to him (we will discuss surrender in the next chapter). Accepting our Father in heaven in this light, it is easier to learn to obey him and learn what we must do to gain favor with him. We cannot talk about our Father in heaven without addressing these three controversial topics.

Obedience is something that is drilled into us as children but of which we usually have a tendency to disregard when we get into our teen and early adult years. We learn to believe that we are able to take care of ourselves and make our own decisions, independent of our parents or anyone else, and so we see no need for obedience any longer.

Obedience is not just kid stuff. It is a value, a character trait up with the primary standards of honesty, trustworthiness, honor, and respect, but it is something that many adults in today's world disregard as childishness. Disobedience, or the disregard of rules (or commandments), causes discord and chaos, and opposes the nature of God. Rules of decency have been disregarded for decades to the point where there is little decency left.

Obedience is much more than simply doing what you are told. There is great honor, humility, and respect in obedience. It is a characteristic of equity. Discernment is part of obedience, knowing who to obey and who not to obey. Obedience does not dictate a blind obedience because that is foolish and is not equitable. Knowing who is and is not your head and submitting yourself, your actions, and your will to that head, obeying all that has been commanded, places you in a position to gain great favor from that superior.

Our Father in heaven and Jesus Christ are our superiors and from whom we seek favor. Submitting to them is the most empowering thing we can do. Obedience to God's law places us in a position to gain favor with God, who helps us to do many things here in this life and in the next. But it all begins with our willingness to obey.

> "My son, forget not my law; but let thine heart keep my commandments: for length of days, and long life, and peace, shall they add to thee. Let not mercy and truth forsake thee: bind them about thy neck; write them upon the table of thine heart: *so shalt thou find favour and good understanding in the sight of God and man.*" (Proverbs 3:1–4 KJV, italics added)

> "A good man obtaineth favour of the Lord; but a man of wicked devices will be condemned." (Proverbs 12:2 KJV)

While the subject of gaining favor with God may make you uncomfortable, it is something that you need to understand. Gaining favor with God is not the inequitable state that you may think. Favor with God is not favoritism. It is equitable because all those who place themselves in this position may gain favor with him. It is good for you to know what you do to find favor with God and what you do to lose it. Knowing it gives you a clear choice. It is a concept that is easy to understand. Those of you who have more than one child, or know someone who does, will understand it easily.

Children often test rules. They test rules as they learn right and wrong, find the accepted boundaries of behavior, and figure out how far they can go from them without consequences. Children learn what is and is not allowed by enforced rules. Sometimes parents spend a great deal of time standing over a child to get them to do... anything. Sometimes even mealtime can be a chore. Usually these are the children who end up accusing one or both of their parents of favoritism toward other siblings. The only thing they saw was that someone else got more than what they did, regardless of their disobedience to the parents' rules.

Parents do not discipline a child who is obedient to the rules, but only disciplines a child whose behavior is unacceptable to the standards set by the parent. Discipline is usually by the suffering of consequences, chastisements, or loss of privileges, and may require punishments if the child does not learn, or ignores, the previous consequences, also set by the parent. While the parent loves all of their children with all the love they can possess, favor is given to the child(ren) who remains in line with acceptable behaviors and set rules. There is no bias against one child and preference to the other(s), but an obedient child is simply easier to raise and the parent can trust the child to do what they know and should do. The difficult and disobedient child would be able to do all of the things that the obedient one does if they had behaved similarly. The negative or positive consequences of the child's behavior attempts to teach the child.

Accepting this concept, we understand our Father in heaven better. Favor is given when we obey the Father's commands, and consequences are given for disobedience. Protections and blessings are given or removed equitably based on the individual's obedience, yet our Father in heaven wants to give favor and blessings to all of his children.

The choices we make, our faith in Jesus, and the importance we place on our obedience to God's commands, within our hearts (not what we have achieved), dictate the level of favor we have with God. Yet we have our agency to do as we desire and act according to our will.

Obedience is a requirement to create a close relationship with God and develop life-changing faith. As you learn to hear and recognize the voice of the Spirit and obey the messages given, you are taught to fine tune your behaviors to act according to God's will—God will prompt you to know what behaviors are acceptable and unacceptable in his eyes. Inasmuch as you heed his promptings, he will continue to instruct you.

Obedience helps you to experience the two-sided relationship with your Father in heaven and Savior that you desire.

Ignoring the voice of your Father in heaven and Savior shows that they are not important to you. It is disrespectful and the Spirit will withdraw from you. Obedience is that important. You cannot create a deep and trusting relationship with them, no matter how much they want to create it with you, if you do not follow their instructions. You will only receive wisdom after you have obeyed. This is key.

To obey God's commands, we need to understand his word. There is a word in the Bible that is not used very often but of which we need to understand in order for us to obey. The word *inasmuch* is an interesting word and one that we must highlight in our Bibles. *Inasmuch*, when understood, offers so much meaning to commandments from our Father in heaven and their association to blessings or consequences.

Inasmuch is a word that means that you receive a reward and consequence on a sliding scale according to your obedience and disobedience to the command. What this means is that if you obey the command one-quarter of the way, you receive one-quarter of a blessing for your obedience and three-quarters of the consequence; halfway, you will receive half of the blessing and half of the consequence, which means that you receive nothing because if you receive half of the blessing and have half of the blessing taken away, as a consequence, you have forfeited the blessing and the consequence, receiving nothing. Put forth some effort to obey the command and you receive a greater reward and little or none of the consequence. In your Bible, replace the word *inasmuch* with the words "to whatever degree that you...."

> "Inasmuch as ye have done it unto one of the least of these my brethren, ye have done it unto me." (Matthew 25:40 KJV)

Jesus' well-known words illustrate the clarification and understanding that the word *inasmuch* offers. Look at the sliding scale. " 'To whatever degree that you' have done it (disregarded or regarded, disrespected or respected, was cruel or kind, whatever *it* is) to any one of my poorest and humblest followers, you have done it unto me." This is Jesus' warning that our judgment will be reflected largely on how we treat people, particularly the poor, the humble, and the meek—and he is very aware of them. Whatever degree we assist or injure one another, we assist or injure Christ and we shall be judged accordingly because he has taken all their suffering on himself.

Inasmuch is so powerful and so important to understand. Pay attention to this word in your Bible and ensure that you clearly understand what it says. Understanding this word offers warnings to prevent the forfeit of blessings simply by not understanding and obeying the command.

When we learn to obey God, we gain more of his favor. Looking at Bible stories, we see those like Moses, Abraham, Job, and others who had the favor of God, and the amazing blessings that they gained. Once we have become favored with God, he generously blesses us, and he orchestrates situations and circumstances to bless us with our greatest desires—even though we may not see that there is a way.

You will feel the Spirit powerfully, and gain confidence as you learn about God. These experiences will teach you to recognize his voice. By obeying your Father in heaven's commands, he will show his great mercy and patience with you because you have illustrated your desire to have Jesus as your God and King. You will learn where you stand with him because you will receive the amazing rewards that he gives, from your obedience.

4

GOD'S WILL AND OUR FAITH

"But without faith it is impossible to please him: for he that cometh to God must believe that he is, and that he is a rewarder of them that diligently seek him."
(Hebrews 11:6 KJV)

How does God's will fit into your faith? That is an interesting question. I listen to people talk. That is one of my…gifts (perhaps curiosities?). I believe that people will tell you everything you need to know about them if you listen to what they say when they do not know you are really listening; the things they communicate but do not say, in words. Listening to people talk about faith, I have found that there are two basic thoughts. Mainly, people talk about God's will as if it is destiny or fate. They talk as if the occurrence, or the result of their circumstance, is God's will and so there is nothing more that they can do. On the other hand, they beg God for what they want or need, promising to change, to do better, or to just be different, to receive that for which they pray, never doing anything more than waiting to see if they receive their requested blessing before being better, different, or doing what was promised, and then forgetting about the whole thing. Then, in their desperation, they do both, trying to find some way to bend God's will to their own so that he gives them the blessing they need or want, promising never to bother him again, ending up believing that there must be no God.

What do we really believe? Do we really believe that we have no power to ask and receive the blessings that we need or want? Do we believe that we can negotiate with anything we have, are, or do, to entice God to give us the things for which we pray? Do we really feel that we need to change his mind? What makes us mere humans think that we have the ability, even necessity, to control God's will? On the other hand, do we really believe that we are powerless? Do we accept that our faith is nothing more than the power to beg, plead, promise, and give up? Perhaps we are so confused by it all that we desperately try to do something, hoping that God hears us and helps us in some way (that is what I did). Yet that is not faith either.

Many mistakenly think that faith is the belief that we must hold our hopes so firmly and unwaveringly that God aligns his will with ours; and yet, in the same breath, we speak as if we are vulnerable to the powers of the universe that are against us. It sounds ridiculous when spelled out, does it not?

In truth, faith is far simpler and more profound than this. The truth is that God's will is not fated. God is able to do all things. When it comes to it, the only things that we can offer are our will, our faith, and our love; even so, God does not need these things. Yet, God's will does not negate our faith. So I ask again, how does God's will fit into our faith?

To gain the most clarity possible about where God's will fits into our faith or how our faith fits in God's will, we need to separate the will of God from our own will, in our minds, because they are two separate things. It does not matter how you look at it, God's will is his alone. We have no more governing power over the will of God than we have power over the sun or stars. To think that we can influence God's will by holding a firm and unwavering hope is arrogant on our part. That is not faith. It is ours, as imperfect beings, to surrender our will to his perfect will, not the other way around; and that includes trying to talk him into, or convince him of, anything.

Ancient Israel's demand for a king illustrates this point perfectly. God warned the people that it would be a bad idea to have a human king when God was their king, but the people demanded and Saul was willing, so God allowed them to have their way. While Saul reigned perfectly for a few years, he became prideful and began doing all that

God had warned Israel that a mortal king would do, and it ended in disaster (see 1 Samuel 8:19 KJV).

God will never usurp his authority over your choice, but if you make the wrong choice and choose your will over his, he will leave you to your own devices and allow the destruction that he foresees (yes, I learned this the hard way).

So, what we are left with, after separating God's will from ours…, is our will. What do we do with our own will? We surrender it to God's perfect will and understanding, if we are wise. Yet we should not simply surrender and not ask for his wisdom, advice, help, or blessings. To do so would also be foolish, for it does not teach us any understanding, and sometimes God is the only one who can help. The only way to learn about God's ways is to gain wisdom from him.

> "For my thoughts are not your thoughts, neither are your ways my ways, saith the Lord. For as the higher are higher than the earth, so are my ways higher than your ways, and my thoughts than your thoughts… and it shall prosper in the thing whereto I sent it." (Isaiah 55:8-9, 11 KJV)

> "As for God, his way is perfect…. It is God that girdeth me with strength, and maketh my way perfect feet, and setteth me upon my high places." (Psalms 18:30, 32 KJV)

Man's ways are not God's ways and God's ways are not man's ways. What we believe may be opposite of reality or wisdom. Man sees wisdom and intelligence as complications and complexities, where God understands that true wisdom only comes by understanding simplicities. Man sees surrender as weakness; where God understands that to surrender to his will teaches man to become like his Son, which in turn offers the power and ability to do all things, through Christ. Man sees happiness as a temporary and fleeting emotion that must be renewed (usually through the purchasing of bigger and better things); where God understands that true happiness comes from the peace and faith in his Son and the assurance of returning to him to receive rewards in heaven, which will bring us and him our greatest joys. Man sees that he must appear perfect, where God understands that to honestly repent of one's sins actually perfects him. Man sees power as pride, dominance, force, intimidation, and cunningness; where God understands that true power only comes through gentleness, meekness, love, honesty, humility, mercy, patience, and acceptance (which is different than tolerance, and also requires discernment to accept truth). Man sees that the ultimate goal of this life is to control his destiny, gain great wealth, and leave a financial inheritance for his children; where God sees that the ultimate goal of this life is to accept Christ as our Savior, discipline ourselves to follow his example, surrender our will to him, and leave a legacy of faith and testimony for generations.

Faith, trust, surrender, and obedience, in and to God, position us to reap great blessings and a place for redemption, salvation, and a reward in the eternities to come. These four attitudes bring us far closer to perfection (and life-changing faith) than all other traits we can gain. Until we are perfected, in the next life, we cannot understand all things as God does. We can, however, begin to learn the beautiful simplicity of truth, and accept that God knows what is best for us. Only by and through our Savior, Jesus Christ, do we have the hope of salvation and a reward in the life to come. He is our only hope.

Now that we have separated God's will from our own (all we need is an awareness and acceptance that God's will is his and our will is ours and they are both separate), we are in a position to request righteous desires. Our hearts and minds are in a place where we may be guided to that which God sees is best for us. It may be years down the road when we receive our desires, or instantly. It may be something that is even better than the blessings that we requested. By accepting God's will as perfect and separate from our will, places our desires in position to be granted in God's way and in God's time, which makes the blessing better and more perfect than we could imagine. We do not truly understand that God knows best, wanting something now, when surrendering to God's ways, means, and timing brings us the perfect blessing.

Some may think that if God does not instantaneously bless us with the blessings we request that he has delayed answering our prayers or has denied our requests. He has not. Sometimes, natural forces must take their natural course, being pushed one way or another as an answer to our prayers. A healing from a disease, for example, may take its natural course but may have been flipped toward healing instead of continuing down its current course toward illness or death. A switch flipping from getting worse to healing is still a healing blessing and is no less than an instantaneous one. Because a switch has been flipped, steering a disease toward healing, it may be better for the patient to have to follow its natural course toward health. That is certainly different from the disease worsening. Surrendering our will to God's will, we also surrender our timing and means to him.

God's will is his, but we can gain the knowledge of what he desires for us in all areas of our lives. By separating his will from our own, surrendering to his will in all things and requesting for his wisdom, we are able to attain the simple requirements of faith, without fear (while surrendering to God's will is not a requirement of faith, as you develop life-changing faith you will desire to surrender your will to him, as he partners with you, to bless your life).

Surrendering your will to God is not usually something that can be done in a moment. It is a process. It requires help from him, as a partner (and is when I learned that he will actually partner with me). Surrendering your will to God is an act of agency. You literally will yourself to surrender to him, letting go a little bit more with each act of will. When you do, you will feel the power of these next two verses, and they become very real and vivid in your life:

> "Fear thou not; for I am with thee: be not dismayed; for I am thy God: I will strengthen thee; yea, I will help thee; yea, I will uphold thee with the right hand of my righteousness. For I the Lord thy God will hold thy right hand, saying unto thee, Fear not; I will help thee." (Isaiah 41:10, 13 KJV)

> "Behold, I have graven thee upon the palms of my hands; thy walls are continually before me." (Isaiah 49:16 KJV)

These are the verses that the Savior showed me just before I finally surrendered to him. These very tender verses convinced me that there is nothing to lose in fully surrendering to the Lord—he is worthy of our trust. It was my own sense of control that kept me from surrendering, more than anything. But he showed me that I was not really in control, and that knowledge gave me the ability to fully surrender. I was holding tight to something I did not have anyway. From my journal, after I fully surrendered to God:

"I again began to pray, not all-together silently, and was able to break through the barriers and fully sacrificed my will to my God. The pain was real and intense, as I poured out my heart's desire to have the feelings of joy, faith, and peace of which I read in the Bible—I *need* that in my life. I want it more than anything else on Earth. I want to have faith and to trust my Savior completely, and I am fully committed to do whatever it takes to get to that point, and beyond. As I sat there, willing to surrender, holding onto my Bible, I opened its pages again and read the pages that opened. I read verses Isaiah 41:10, 13. There was also a bookmark in that page upon which had the verse Isaiah 49:16. In tears, I said aloud, 'I cannot keep doing this. It is too hard! Anything I do is … not doing any good!'

"So with tears in my eyes, I let go and surrendered. It took about four or five times to truly surrender—I mean all of it. I could feel me give up and give it all to him. And then something happened that I had never felt before. The feelings of joy I experienced, as I fully surrendered, were amazing! It was very similar to feelings I experienced when I repent and gain a release and forgiveness from my sins—yes, that is what it was… relief, but it was bigger. I know that my prayer pleased God—I can feel it. What an amazing and empowering experience. Thank you, Father!"

It is difficult to describe how I felt—my experience and what changed when I finally surrendered to God—but I will try. I know that the Spirit had guided me to that point. There were hints that led me to that place. I had been on my mission for a couple of months now and was working with the people I served. I had difficulties at every turn. It started with inane things like silly accusations to which I had to answer, but it quickly escalated to the point where I was accosted and my life threaten—and she was serious. When several serious and frightening things happened, all in the same week, I was done and could not deal with any more. That was when I was compelled to give it all to God— my way was not working, anyway. It was Jesus' mission, not mine. He asked this of me and so I knew that if he wanted me to continue, he would provide ways for me to complete it. So I gave up trying my way. I let go of my ego, my stubbornness, my will, and my life, giving it all to Jesus. I surrendered to what he wanted: my life to continue or allow the woman to take it, as long as Jesus willed it.

That Sunday, as I stood before the choir for choir practice (I was a church's choir director), I saw that she was there—the woman who had threatened my life! Was this the day she was going to kill me? Would it be in the chapel? I remembered that my life was not my own and that I was on Jesus' mission. After choir practice the woman approached me. I tried to breathe as she summoned me.

I do not know exactly what happened, but the threats ceased... and she kept attending choir practice. When she spoke to me, it was to question how to do something regarding music. It was as if she forgot who I was—and also all the people with whom she associated forgot too. It was over. She was a changed woman and she was able to feel the Spirit of Christ, as she sang, for I saw tears stream from her eyes on more than one occasion, as we performed.

Although I do not remember her name, over the years, I will never forget her, and I still see her face in my memories. God bless this woman!

While I do not know what exactly will happen when you surrender your will to God (if anything), for me, things changed. The Spirit became my guide and teacher. Things jumped out on the pages of my Bible that I had never heard or read before but they were clearer and more understandable. I began to understand that there is no reason to do anything alone or without consulting him—I am dependent on him, anyway. There are no trivial matters in this life. Even things that are disappointing, like the desire for sin, felt more natural to take to him. Our Father in heaven and Savior became full and senior partners in my life as I begin to fully trust and rely on them in all things—and you will feel that, too.

> "But as many as received him, to them he gave the right to become children of God, even to those who believe in his name: who were born, not of blood, nor of the will of the flesh, nor of the will of man, but of God." (John 1:12–13 KJV, see also Psalms 82:6 KJV)

God showed me this verse one morning. Through this partnership between you and deity, you are given the ability to see yourself as a son or daughter of God, and be able to accept and feel it. That knowledge will be beautiful and powerful in your life. It will help you to have the courage to set healthy boundaries in relationships, not allowing them to undermine your understanding as God's child. You will have the courage to end relationships that harm your peace and your spirit (toxic relationships), those who try to keep you bound to the last big mistake that you made and not giving allowances for forgiveness, growth, or anything else. You will make decisions that are healthy, empowering, and more in line with God's will for you because he will teach and guide you to the good things, and rid you of the bad. You will feel that God loves you and no person can take that away from you.

If you do not completely trust God today, tell him that you want to trust him. Feel the desire—experience the emotions of your desire until you actually can trust him. As you continue to tell him, your level grows and deepens until you are able to get on your knees and tell him that you trust him in a crisis, which is far more trust than you have ever had before. That will give you the ability to see, like young David, the great blessings and protections that he has provided for you in the past, and then you will let go and trust him completely, and your life will change forever.

God's will is his alone. Understanding and accepting this, we recognize that he is God, omnipotent (all power), omniscient (all knowing), and omnipresent (in all places), and this is the position we need to be in to learn to ask for blessings from him without the begging, pleading, and promising, which simply never worked anyway. Understanding and accepting that God's will is his alone, we are also in position to truly have faith in Christ, the faith that works, and the faith the changes your life.

5

WORTHINESS

"That ye might walk worthy of the Lord unto all
pleasing, being fruitful in every good work, and
increasing in the knowledge of God."
(Colossians 1:10 KJV)

Feelings of unworthiness are the biggest roadblocks to developing life-changing faith. Faith is a principle that requires worthiness, yet feelings of unworthiness can keep us bound to a mediocre level of faith, if it can develop at all. Because many do not feel that they are worthy of faith, they are subsequently kept from the blessings from our Father in heaven, which causes more feelings of unworthiness because of our agency. It is an evil cycle.

Many believe that to be worthy they must be perfect or very close to it. They believe that they must keep their lives in constant religious piety to obtain blessings from God. Guilt associated with feelings of unworthiness and simple misunderstandings about what worthiness is, stops many from developing faith.

One of the most common reasons that we feel unworthy is that we blend words and meanings, using them interchangeably. In various parts of the country and throughout the world, people take the meaning of one word and put it to another, not understanding its true meaning. People in different regions (and even of a state) can misuse a word or mispronounce it in common communication, which causes confusion, especially when speaking with someone who is not from that region.

Many times we cross meanings or definitions to words, believing that they mean something other than what the word actually means.

I learned this concept very early in my life. Many of my family members use *varely* for the word *barely*, even pronouncing it the same but with a 'v.' In one of my high school English classes, I tried to write *varely* in a short story. I tried to figure out how to spell it and realized that I had never written it before. Thinking about it some more, I realized that I had not even read it; I had only heard it spoken. I went into the back of the room and looked for the word in the dictionary, looking through all words starting with a 'v,' and saw that it was not there—*verily* was there but not *varely*. I knew that it meant the same thing as *barely* but... then it struck me. The word was not an actual word but something that was said by family, from the region where they were from. Many years later, I had the opportunity to live for ten months in the southern part of the state and heard *varely* said everywhere. It was something that my grandparents said and taught to their children because it was common language from that area.

Speaking specifically about the word *worthy*, we often confuse it with the word *deserving*, thinking that it means the same thing, just like I did, in my writing class. We believe that if we are worthy, we would have achieved a higher level of righteousness to receive more blessings, being more deserving of them at that advanced level. We believe that our faith will automatically grow once we are more deserving of greater faith. We do not understand that *deserving* and *worthy* are not the same.

The word *deserving* is a word of achievement. It means to earn something, to be entitled, getting what is owed. The word *deserving* refers to something of our own doing—an accomplishment. While there may be elements of worthiness in deservedness, we can still be worthy while we are struggling and failing to deserve, because we have not been perfected in this life.

There is nothing in this life that we can do, as imperfect beings, to deserve the blessings we receive from God. The only man that deserved anything from the Father was Jesus, and that was because of all that he had done and achieved *before* he came to Earth, *before* he lived his mortal life, and he had sound understanding and did not err, in his life.

Where the word *deserving* holds a level of achievement that is unattainable, the word *worthy* places us in a position to receive blessings from our loving Father in heaven. The word *worthy* is a position of *blamelessness*; of *satisfaction, delight,* and *pleasure*; being *true, upright,* and *honorable.* Allow this to sink into your heart and understanding. The word *worthy* means *valuable, precious, estimable, credible,* and *of great worth.*

We can only deserve blessings from God after we have been sanctified and perfected by the blood of the atonement—in the next life. But Jesus created the bridge between us and God so that we may be worthy in God's eyes now, in our imperfect state. Because of Jesus, we may be worthy in spite of our shortcomings and sins. Belief in Jesus Christ and committing to follow his ways, no matter how well we are able to actually emulate him, makes us credible with God inasmuch as we strive (try) to obey God's commandments. Furthermore, being willing to be obedient to God's commands makes us even more credible, and brings the Father greater pleasure and satisfaction, thereby making us more worthy.

There are no demands of perfection or even achievement in the word *worthy.* Worthiness is in our belief, the direction we are facing and moving toward, Jesus or Satan, no matter how slowly we move or how many times we trip and fall. Worthiness is not in the achievement, but in the trying—in the struggle. Understanding the differences in these two words helps us to see that we may be worthy of the blessings that God has in store for us while we are traveling toward deserving—in the next life.

We see that life's road is much like a mountainous path. There are parts of the path that have a steep grade (repentance), loose and large rocks (deception and temptation) that we need to maneuver around, and there are even large tree roots (false beliefs) in our path to trip us. But our Savior has built a bridge for us. He has bridged these faulty paths and has given us the ability to walk in smooth, firmly packed soil (forgiveness) and grassy meadows (blessings). You may even come into a beautiful meadow filled with fragrant flowers (miracles), or you may come to the edge of a cliff (sin), and if you get too close to temptation you may either fall off its edge or come close to it; but he has a bridge or ladder (repentance and forgiveness) for these too.

No matter where you are on your path when you are taken from this life, whenever that may be, if you are facing in the direction of the Lord and are trying to move toward him, even if you have just fallen off the cliff of sin, and are repenting and trying to make your way back to where you once were, you may be considered worthy because of the direction of your heart. Of course, there may be cliffs that are big enough that the fall may break your leg (religious probation), land you in the hospital (church disfellowshipment), or in the intensive care unit (church excommunication). These sins put you out of commission for a while to heal, but the Savior's atonement closes that gap between you and your Father in heaven there, as well. You still have the choice which direction you face on your path—toward the Savior or in any other direction. There may still be consequences, legally, in your church, etc., and you may lose the ability to have the Spirit with you for a while, but you still have the choice as to which direction you face and how you will handle it. Your direction dictates your worthiness. The desires of your heart set your direction on your life path and therefore, your worthiness (or your ability to be worthy again, after being forgiven from your sins).

We see both ends of David's experiences (the faith of young David when he took up river stones to fight against the giant, Goliath; and his sin with Bath-Sheba, and his plan and execution to hide his sin by having her husband killed). Even with all that David had done throughout his life, even with the harsh and painful consequences of sin, he praised God throughout the rest of his life, singing psalms and continuing to write about God's great mercies. David walked a rocky road on his life path (he learned the whole spectrum of human experience), and while he could have become embittered through his pain and loss, which was extensive, he set the course of his life path toward the Savior and patiently waited for forgiveness, with the hope that he would eventually receive it.

It really is about the intentions of your heart. As long as you are facing the Savior, wanting to please him and trying to keep your Father's commandments, no matter how well you can actually do them, you are counted as (or working toward) worthy simply because you are facing and focusing on Jesus. You are worthy because your heart is his. You are worthy because you are trying. You are worthy because you continue to struggle with your human nature. This means that you are indeed worthy of God's great love and blessings.

I turn to the life of the Savior many times to get his perfect perspective on many gospel topics. Understanding that Jesus provided us with a perfect example gives us the reassurance that we will receive truth. Because I have had so many false beliefs, throughout my life, I prayerfully rely on my Bible and answers from my Savior to show me the way. Anything that I do not find in this sacred record, I simply let go, knowing that I will gain the truth and correction in the next life, as all of us will. We do not need to know all things now. Those things that we do need to know now will be given by the Spirit.

Never in any of the miracles recorded in the Bible did Jesus ever ask for proof of the recipient's worthiness as a condition to be healed by him. He did not stop the woman who had hemorrhaged (issue of blood) for twelve years, who was healed when she touched the hem of his garment, to ask her to provide any information regarding her worthiness. He stopped only to see the person who had held such strong faith in him as to draw power from him.

This story has so much hidden meaning that we do not receive by simply reading the account. The woman had an *issue of blood*, a kind of hemorrhage that did not heal for twelve long years (we do not know why she hemorrhaged for twelve years, whether it was due to a blood disease, like hemophilia, or perhaps a physiological problem after childbirth or other female condition). She had gone to several physicians, spending all of her money, to find a cure but no physician could heal her.

The problem with bleeding for twelve years is not only an issue for her health, which would have been extensive, leaving her weak and anemic, but it was also a legal issue, too. The Hebrew Law (Leviticus 15 KJV) clearly listed a person with an *issue of blood*, no matter the cause, as an unclean person. This woman would have not been allowed into the city, living with lepers and other *unclean* people who were to live outside of the city walls. For the twelve years of her *banishment*, for a lack of a better word, she was unable to receive help from family and friends, in her weakened condition, because God's law clearly stated that anyone who touches or is touched by an unclean person, touches anything that was touched by an unclean person, or even walks where an unclean person walked, would be unclean themselves. Of course, the Law stated that their defilement would only last until the evening and would require the washing of their bodies and their clothes but, understanding human nature, it would have been taken to the extreme.

This woman, who would not be able to walk, in her extremely weakened condition, on the day that Jesus came to her city, made her way into the city (the first no-no) and touched the hem of Jesus' robe (the second no-no), thinking that no one would be the wiser. But Jesus noticed. He noticed, even with of the hundreds of people in the city, that day. He noticed, even though the crowd pressed and pushed around him. The awareness that someone had touched him with the faith to be healed stopped him in his tracks.

Jesus stopped and turned around to see the frightened and feeble woman, crouching into the doorway to let her know that she was noticed, of all of the people surrounding him; and he stopped to explain to her plainly that it was her faith in him that healed her. That is correct. She healed herself through her faith in Jesus—the bridge between us and God. He only wanted to see the woman who had such great faith in him. He never asked her about how righteous or how close to perfection she was—even though he would have known that she was *unclean*. The people around him would have gasped at the nerve of this *unclean* woman who had come into the city *and* touched Jesus. But there was no interview, even then. There was no interview before he healed anyone. Never, not once. The Savior simply blessed all who came to him; in spite of the Law (Jesus knew that he was the new law). He never turned anyone away. He never refused to bless anyone. These next verses clearly state that Jesus heals all who come unto him:

> "And to him that is near, saith the Lord; I will heal him." (Isaiah 57:19 KJV)

> "Now when the sun was setting, all they that had any sick with divers diseases brought them unto him; and he laid his hands on every one of them, and healed them." (Luke 4:40 KJV, see also Mark 1:34 KJV and Matthew 8:16 KJV)

If the Savior blessed people so openly and willingly when he was on the earth, why do you think that he will not bless your life as openly and willingly now? Do you really believe that he would negatively change his willingness to bless people's lives today? There is a reason you do not believe that Jesus will not bless you now. What do you believe?

In our desires for light and knowledge, we complicate so much of the gospel with things that do not pertain to the simple nature of gospel principles. We get stuck in our false beliefs, waiting for a chance to bind us with doubt. Many times we believe that earthly standards of excellence belong in Godly matters and unfortunately, there are earthly people who would support such ideas. We build gospel principles larger and more dynamic than they truly are, which make some appear intelligent and learned, by worldly standards, but which cause confusion for all those who listen. We create perplexing commentaries to simple gospel principles that make them complicated, where true gospel principles are freeing and clarifying, because of their simplicity. We debate scriptural truths to prove that the other person is wrong, and we are right (just like the Pharisees and the Sadducees, in Jesus' time). Adding complications to simplicity is a matter of pride, not righteousness.

When we look for complexities in the gospel, we will find them (seek and ye shall find), but this is where understanding and clarity is taken from us and we are left in the confusion that we have created. We desire that simplicity is more difficult so that we feel inequitably more deserving or more righteous than others. We desire that we feel that we have earned our salvation in some way. If we desire or focus on complications to gospel principles, God will allow it so that we may stumble, *seeking* being an act of will. If we focus on wanting to earn our reward in heaven, we will find that it is impossible to do so, for "NO... unclean person ...hath any inheritance in the Kingdom of Christ and of God" (Ephesians 5:5 KJV, capitals added; see also Revelation 21:27). Being imperfect beings, we cannot earn a reward in heaven. The grace of our Savior's atoning sacrifice is our only hope for salvation, which choice is equitably given to all men freely, whether they choose to take advantage of it or not.

This means, however, that the opposite applies as well. If we seek to understand the simplicity of the gospel of Jesus Christ, we shall also find it, and it shall become beautiful and powerful in our minds. Our focus must be on Christ and in obedience to God's commands, not on seeking to be viewed as spiritually intelligent by other imperfect humans.

Wherever you are in your understanding, knowledge, belief or disbelief, if you are facing toward Jesus and have repented of your sins (for God cannot even look upon you when you are still guilty of sin, refusing to repent, for whatever reason), you are worthy of blessings from God. Where you are on your path is where you are because that is as far as your understanding has taken you. And it is good. You are only held accountable for your own understanding of truth and the misconceptions you have willfully created or have adopted as truth and refuse to change. If you have accepted Jesus as your Savior, are striving to be like him, and have repented and received a forgiveness of your sins, you are worthy and nobody can take that away from you, but you.

The well-known passage about the Good Shepherd should read more clearly with the correct understanding of worthiness:

> "They that are whole have no need of a physician, but they that are sick: I came not to call the righteous, but sinners to repentance." (Mark 2:17 KJV)

Followed by these verses:

> "For the Son of man is come to save that which was lost. How think ye? If a man have an hundred sheep, and one of them be gone astray, doth he not leave the ninety and nine, and goeth into the mountains, and seeketh that which is gone astray? And if so be that he find it, verily I say unto you, he rejoiceth more of that sheep, than of the ninety and nine which went not astray. Even so it is not the will of your Father which is in heaven, that one of these little ones should perish." (Matthew 18:11–14 KJV)

We are all sinners, but these verses have far more insight than simply to say that all people are sinners. Jesus came to the earth to save us all from our sins—large and small, grievous and trite. Those who firmly walk the path of righteousness are left to tend themselves. He came not to call the righteous to repentance unless they go astray, but he calls the sinners to repentance to bring those who have lost their way, back to God.

We are all sinners, but not all disciples of Christ are in need of a shepherd to constantly keep them in the flock. Many understand that wandering off the path toward Jesus brings us unhappiness and suffering, and so have disciplined them to remain on the path and close to the flock. These are those who are found each week in churches, and at other times throughout the week. These are also those who may not be found in churches but know that Jesus is the king of their hearts and worship in their own ways (Jesus knows his people). The Good Shepherd leaves those who are able to tend themselves and goes after those who have strayed or cannot find the flock in the first place, so that they may partake of the goodness that the gospel of Jesus Christ brings.

Some very worthy followers of Christ feel unworthy of the blessings that God has for them because they feel that they are not doing all that they think they are supposed to do. We do not need to do all things at all stages of our lives. Our entire lives encompass all of the things that we are required to do. The Bible explains:

> "To every thing there is a season, and a time to every purpose under heaven: A time to be born, and a time to die; a time to plant, and a time to pluck up that which is planted; a time to kill, and a time to heal; a time to break down, and a time to build up; a time to weep and a time to laugh; a time to mourn, and a time to dance; a time to cast away stones, and a time to gather stones together; a time to embrace, and a time to refrain from embracing; a time to get, and a time to lose; a time to keep, and a time to cast away; a time to rend, and a time to sew; a time to keep silence, and a time to speak; a time to love, and a time to hate; a time of war, and a time of peace." (Ecclesiastes 3:1–8 KJV)

In our world, it may look like this: a time for raising one's children and a time for being alone with one's spouse (or alone), a time to read Bible stories and a time for an in-depth study, a time to worship as a family and a time to worship alone. There are many other things that we may add to this list. God has provided whatever time he has allotted to each of us for all that we need to accomplish. The rest will simply be understood by him or corrected, or we will be asked to account for our failings. But remember that a willing heart accounts for most of the things we were not able to accomplish; because we were willing (willingness is an act of agency). Listen for promptings from the Spirit and follow them. Listening and following promptings are the most important things that we can do, anyway.

Do not fear about what you *should* be doing. You do not need to run faster than you are able. It is all about balance. Give allowances to yourself and others. Learn to hear (not only listen, but actually hear, which comes from the heart) and then see through the eyes of compassion, patience, and mercy (like Jesus does). Understand that people, for the most part, are simply trying to live their lives the best way they can. What you see though biased view is not truth. I urge you to not judge—you or others. Only Jesus can judge accurately, and he will tell you what you need to do.

I caution you that those who have wandered and have had the Good Shepherd rescue them are those who have experienced the Savior's love in their lives, personally. Know that we all have some misconceptions and false beliefs that need to be changed, but some may be so severe that they require rescue from the Good Shepherd. Those who stay close to the flock may miss opportunities to hear from the most amazing blessings of Jesus' love, which they would miss hearing about, otherwise. Humans cannot judge whether or not someone is worthy of God's love because we are all sinners. Our perceptions have corrupted truth. The second that someone turns toward Christ and are forgiven of their sins, they are worthy in God's eyes and may be more worthy than those who unrighteously judge, no matter your thoughts about them.

It would surprise many to learn that the most spiritual places on Earth are not in churches, temples, university-level religion classes, or not even in homes during Bible studies. The most spiritual places on

Earth are in prison chapels. While the Spirit may be in your Sabbath chapel worship meetings, Jesus himself is in prison chapels, sitting next to men and women who have made mistakes, some large and grave ones, and are experiencing Jesus' love for the first time. I knew a woman who was a missionary in a woman's prison who told me several times that "where God may not be in prison chapels (because God cannot even look on sin with any approval), you definitely find Jesus there, and his Spirit is abundant and powerful, far more so than any church I have attended outside." It begs for me to say again that many of these hardened criminals may be more worthy of God's love than those who may be sitting in church pews, unrighteously judging them.

> "If ye were of the world, the world would love his own: but because ye are not of the world, but I have chosen you out of the world, therefore the world hateth you. Remember the word that I said unto you, The servant is not greater than his lord. If they have persecuted me, they will also persecute you; if they have kept my saying, they will keep yours also. But all these things will they do unto you for my name's sake, because they know not him that sent me." (John 15:19–21 KJV)

> "Verily I say unto you, Inasmuch as ye have done it unto one of the least of these my brethren, ye have done it unto me." (Matthew 25:40 KJV)

To those who judge another, I beg you to ask for forgiveness. We will never know why people do what they do. Only God knows what is in a person's heart. We cannot judge another's motives. We cannot know what they have endured and are currently enduring. And we cannot know what things are happening, the human forces that are hidden and working against them—they may not even know until prejudice is created in those around them and it is too late for them to see (or care about) truth. We can only judge what is in our own minds and hearts, and even that judgment comes from flawed information. Also know that mistakes are not sins. So, we cannot accurately judge.

Whether it is the prison in your own belief system or a physical prison, Jesus is there to find those who have lost their way and those who need healing, no matter whether it is a healing of the body, spirit, heart, or understanding. Jesus will find the lost lambs because they are precious to him and sees that they are in trouble in some way. He finds them in some personal and profound way to bring them to repentance, to heal them, and to bring them home.

Our Savior's precious sacrifice made it possible for us to be worthy by our willingness to do all that we cannot actually do, trying to do better day by day. Our willingness to continue struggling against our sinful natures are pleasing to God and therefore make us worthy of the great blessings and favors that he has for us, no matter where we are in our paths.

I sincerely hope that the light of truth has been shed on the subject of worthiness. If there are still some residual false beliefs about worthiness, please re-read this chapter, making sure to read and ponder the biblical references. Pray about the things that you have learned, and the feelings that you have experienced. Prayerfully discuss these things with God so that you are able to move past any worthiness issues that may keep you from developing life-changing faith. Deception about worthiness is the biggest stumbling block against faith. It was for me, too. It will keep you from believing Jesus, no matter how much you believe in him.

As we continue into the next topic, let us look at all that we have learned about worthiness and check it against our spiritual barometer:

> *Anything that distances you from your Father in heaven and Savior is evil and is from Satan. Truth only holds beliefs that give you a desire to be close to them without fear. You can tell if anything is good or bad by questioning whether it brings you closer to them or takes you further away—for anything that is evil will not bring you closer to your Father in heaven and his Son, where anything that is good will not take you away from them.*

From this chapter, we defined worthiness is being valuable, precious, estimable, credible, and of great worth (rather than anything that we can deserve, requiring achievement), accepting that we are worthy because God gains pleasure in our lives, as we struggle and keep trying to follow Jesus. Does this definition of worthiness bring someone closer to our Father in heaven and his Son, based on our spiritual barometer? Yes, it does. Do you see that this definition helps you to accept that you may be worthy of great and wonderful blessings from God? Yes. Do not listen to the devil any more. Let the guilt dissipate—no, drop it completely. You are worthy.

6

THE POWER TO CHOOSE
RIGHTEOUS DESIRES

**"Butter and honey shall he eat, that he may know
to refuse the evil, and choose the good."
(Isaiah 7:15 KJV)**

Agency is the ability to act according to your will, pleasure, desire, and choice. It is among the three greatest gifts given to you (along with the atonement and the Holy Ghost). Agency is the power given by God to deliberately and intentionally govern your life, through your choices. Intentional ruling and management of your life, through your choices, requires positive and negative consequences to teach you right and wrong. Learning to correctly understand right and wrong, and disciplining yourself to work with the laws of the universe (not against them), helps you to correctly fine tune your decision-making mechanism, and will result in creating a happy and successful life.

Agency has been given to humankind from the beginning. From the beginning, we were given the power to choose for ourselves. The power of choice was so important to our Father in heaven that he gave it to all before the universe was created. It was a foundational principal in universal law. Of course, we know that agency was given to Adam and Eve in the garden. Adam and Eve were commanded not to partake of the fruit of the tree of Knowledge of Good and Evil, which was placed in the far corner of the garden, but were told that they were free to choose. If they chose to seek that tree and break that command, there would be a consequence—death. Death was more than just the ability for their bodies to die, but it was more importantly about a spiritual death, in that they would no longer be able to be in the presence of God and would be distanced from him.

In our day, the Bible serves as warnings to all those who would receive them (an act of agency). There are great many warnings in the Bible regarding our agency and will. Pride and rebellion against God are acts of will, as are humility and submission. Throughout the whole of the Old Testament we see acts of agency that lead to reward or destruction. The stories of David show us great willful acts on both ends of the spectrum.

David showed great faith, as a boy, as he took up river stones to fight the greatest and largest warrior of the Philistine nation, Goliath. Knowing that God had protected him from a bear and a mountain lion, he knew that God would also protect him against Goliath. David showed great faith. Faith is an act of will. Alternatively, later when he sinned with Bathsheba, he set a plan to have her husband, Uriah the Hittite, return from war to lie with her, to hide his sin. When Uriah would not lie with her, out of consideration for the remaining troops still back on the battlefield, David devised another plan to have him killed by putting him on the front lines. Sins and plans to cover those sins are also acts of will. One led to a reward, while the other led to destruction.

Accepting truths or not are also done by our agency. There are many stubborn people who refuse to accept truth even when it is pointed out to them (mostly because of biases against the person who has the truth). Many times, we are left to our own devices simply because we refused truth. Yet, when we accept it, we are liberated from the bonds of the lie.

One of the most powerful Bible stories that illustrate this is the story about the ancient Israelites and the brass serpent. The Israelites walked in the wilderness from Mount Hor, by way of the Red Sea, toward the land of Edom. The people were discouraged because they were back at the Red Sea, where their journey had started. They started to complain about the difficulties they had endured and that they essentially went nowhere. The people complained much, even after all that God had done for them, through their journey. Because they refused to listen to the many chastisements given, God sent fiery serpents (poisonous sand snakes) to humble them. Many died from the serpents' poisonous bites. When they were sufficiently humbled, the people asked Moses to pray to God to take away the serpents. God told Moses to make a brass snake and set it on a pole and everyone who had been bitten would live if they would simply look to it, as we look to Jesus and live (the serpent on the pole symbolized the sting of the crucifixion of Jesus) (Numbers 21: 4–9 KJV, see also John 3:14 KJV). It does not state it, but I wonder how many did not look or merely gave a passing glance, giving up and saying, "See! It did not work."

We cannot completely understand the power of agency the way that God does, but our agency is most important to him. He considers our agency in everything that he does for us. He, the perfect and most powerful God, cannot do anything that goes against our agency. All things honor our power of choice. It is vitally important to developing life-changing faith that you understand this clearly and take it literally. This is key.

Our agency is the most powerful tool that we have. It is through our agency that we gain the desires of our hearts, we claim and accept the atonement, we take the bread and drink (i.e., Communion, Sacrament, Lord's Supper, Eucharist, etc.), sin, repent…, everything. Because agency governs our entire lives, we must willingly and intentionally lay claim to and request blessings from our Father in heaven. God cannot force anything on us that we have not intentionally chosen and requested in some way.

Many mistakenly believe that if God wants to bless our lives, he will do so and therefore if we do not receive blessings, we must not be worthy of them. What we do not understand is that if this was the case, God would bless our lives against our will. In reality, if we do not receive blessings from our Father in heaven, it has a great deal to do with the fact that we do not ask for them or have not requested them in a way that he can give to us.

There are three powerful ways in which we request blessings from heaven and all three of them use our agency: (1) We receive blessings as consequences of obedience to God's commands. God's laws have blessings or consequences associated with obedience or disobedience, based on the degree to which we try or refuse to obey. By ensuring that our hearts' intents and desires are to please God, we may purposefully and intentionally automatically receive blessings from him as consequences of our devotion and obedience. (2) We receive consequences from our energies. All energies have associated consequences, either negative or positive, so our energies either repel or attract blessings to us depending on the types of energies expended. These consequences are due to natural or universal laws. While people mostly think of natural laws as new age philosophy, they were established when the universe was created to assure order. Personally, the natural laws determine our personal successes or failures, depending on our beliefs, thoughts, actions, energies, attitudes, focuses, and the words we use in our daily lives, and accumulate to create the conditions of our lives in the future. We may receive blessings by conforming to these laws by the energies that we send out to the world and universe, especially toward people. (3) We may verbally request blessings. This is the most powerful way to receive blessings. Simply by asking, we may receive them. These three ways were clearly defined and established before the creation. These laws must be obeyed by everyone, including God. God cannot go against his own laws for he created them to keep order in the universe, and going against them would cause chaos.

There are differing opinions on the universal laws, how many and what they are, but all contain the Law of Cause and Effect. The Law of Cause and Effect states that there is a consequence (reaction) to every energy (action) (aka, Newton's 3rd Law of Motion). All action starts a reaction that returns back to you. While Newton was talking about objects, it applies to all energies. Rudeness, for example, begets more rudeness until someone gets hurt. On the other hand, kindness begets more generosity, and respect is extended. Yet, we do not think about the other side of the law—the equal and opposite reaction—it is equally important. Gossip begets listening ears, too, not just the wagging of tongues (you can tell that I abhor gossiping). This equal and opposite reaction can break the chain simply by refusing to listen and telling the gossiper that you do not want to hear it, also setting in motion a different type of energy.

The Law of Cause and Effect not only affects our actions but also entails our thoughts, beliefs, intents, attitudes, desires, focuses, traditions, and all other energies. Whatever energy we put out into the world, particularly toward people, we receive similar energies with increase—100 fold. This includes mercy, judgment, forgiveness, negativity, enthusiasm, insidiousness, backbiting—it includes everything. Many know this law as Karma, while others think about the Golden Rule (Matthew 7:12 KJV). Christians think about Jesus' stark warning: "Verily I say unto you, Inasmuch as ye have done it unto one of the least of these my brethren, ye have done it unto me" (Matthew 25:40 KJV). To place ourselves in a position to receive more positive *effects*, we need to put more positive *causes* out into the world. We need to treat people (and ourselves) with more generosity, kindness, mercy, and forgiveness; and change our beliefs and thoughts into those that will generate more positive consequences and less negative ones.

Understanding that the most powerful way to request blessings from heaven is by praying, what things should we pray for? It makes sense that we pray for righteous desires and not sinful ones. To do so we need to understand exactly what righteous desires are. While we think that we understand them, we may not understand it clearly enough to describe it in words.

Righteous desires are unselfish, service-oriented desires, right? Well, of course, that is true but there are many more righteous desires than those that are service oriented. Many people believe that righteous desires must always be for others. This is not the case. They can be for you and your family members too. This is a common misconception.

Another misconception is that righteous desires must be spiritual or church oriented, that the desire must be about strengthening the faith (e.g., missionary work, bearing witnesses, or sharing spiritual experiences). Righteous desires are not exclusive to those things pertaining to our spiritual lives. God is interested in all aspects of our lives.

Many people think that we cannot ask God for anything that is not known to be his will. They believe that they must wait for a sign (even though we have been told not to look for signs) or receive a list of things that God will allow before they ask for any blessing from him. They misinterpret the meaning "rest in the Lord, and wait patiently for him" (Psalms 37:7 KJV). Many believe that to wait patiently for the Lord means that they must wait for him to tell us what to do and how to do it before deciding on what would be helpful or necessary. They are too afraid that by asking for something that does not align with what they know to be God's will (even though they have never asked his will) and having received a sign indicating such, they would immediately be condemned. Many also believe that they should not ask at all, but wait for God to decide to bless us in his own time. These are common misconceptions and misinterpretations of true messages in the Bible.

Waiting patiently for the Lord does not mean that we wait for him to bless us for things we need and want without asking. In fact, waiting patiently for the Lord has nothing to do with receiving blessings from God at all. Instead, it means that we anticipate his coming, staying on our path toward Christ; we patiently wait for deliverance from our trials, trusting in him throughout, no matter how long he allows us to be tried; and we wait on him like a waiter waits on his customers, waiting and listening to see if he has a request from us, doing it immediately when prompted. In other words, we endure and watch and listen. The Bible instructs us to ask and we shall be given.

What is a righteous desire? That leaves many windows for interpretation and opinion. So, let us look at its opposite: What is a wicked or evil desire? The opposite of the word evil is not selfish, as some may think (am I the only one?). The opposite of righteous is wicked or evil; therefore, the opposite of a righteous desire is an evil one (being equitably selfish is not a sin. We can ask for blessings for us, personally). So, to look at what a wicked or evil desire is provides a clearer understanding of what a righteous one is.

An evil desire would take advantage of a person for gain. That means that a plan or scheme would be set up to create a win/lose situation, whereby one person would be used and suffer a loss so that another can gain unfairly. An evil desire would persuade someone to do evil, break the law, and intentionally harm another person or people. An evil desire would make someone question or deny their belief in Jesus, or would entice and invite someone to sin. An evil desire is something that takes another's agency away by force or through manipulation, deceit, coercion, dishonesty, or insidiousness (this is why gossip is so bad). An evil desire is any of these things done to a child or someone without the capacity to choose for themselves, being innocent.

Along with evil desires, there are other things for which we should not request. We are not to ask for a sign. God gave signs to prophets as tools for his purposes and to show that God was most powerful. The prophets did not request them.

> "An evil and adulterous generation seeketh after a sign; and there shall no sign be given to it." (Matthew 12:39 KJV)

The problem with signs is that they do not develop or increase faith because they provide proof (proof stagnates power, where faith generates and propels it. We need to have both access to Jesus' power [for we cannot do it for ourselves] and the power to make it move through the intentions and earnestness in our hearts). This life is not about proof, it is about faith. There is power in faith that is needed, so to ask for proof is asking to dissolve faith. We need the power that comes with faith in Jesus.

We are also not to ask anything amiss.

> "Ye lust, and have not: ye kill, and desire to have, and cannot obtain: ye fight and war, yet ye have not, because ye ask not. Ye ask, and receive not, because ye ask amiss, that ye may consume it upon your lusts." (James 4:2–3 KJV)

One of the biggest reasons we do not receive blessings is that we are double-minded and we ask things that are amiss. *Amiss* is an interesting word. Asking for anything that is amiss and done with double-mindedness can cause confusion.

The word *amiss* means *wrong, incorrect, unclear, or confusing.* We are not to ask for these things. James instructs us not to ask for things that are amiss, but he specifies more than his simple words suggest. James was clear about not asking for things that would be consumed on our lusts, but he also explained that people will do nearly anything to get the things they want and need, killing, fighting, and hurting others to do so, and still do not receive them because they do not ask

God. Then when they finally ask and still do not receive their desires, it is because they have asked for things that are wrong, things we have already discussed: asking for signs, taking someone's agency, and asking for things that are evil. If we do not understand this completely, we innocently request for things that are amiss, which makes it impossible for our Father in heaven to bless us.

I recall a time when I asked for something for which I should not have asked. I wanted to have such great faith that I could be able to move mountains (sounds like a righteous request, right?). Not that I would actually move mountains, but I wanted my faith to be that strong. I prayed and asked for it and was given a stupor instead (a stupor is a removal of an idea and its associated feelings. I'll teach you more about stupors in the next chapter). I did not know why I received a stupor instead of the faith, at the time. I thought that perhaps I was not ready for such great faith—I did not ask why.

Asking for power when we do not need it goes against what God wants for us. Asking for great power can pull focus away from our Savior and toward a person, which definitely goes against his will. I would learn later that my request was amiss because it was wrong for me to ask for this. Reading my thoughts and emotions, I was really asking for the ability to move mountains, my heart yearning for that type of power. The Spirit later let me know that developing life-changing faith is actually what I really wanted, but my words and feelings said something different. That was the reason why I received the stupor, instead. What I should have asked for was the amount and strength of my faith is such so that I could be able to move mountains, if the situation required it. Developing life-changing faith is the strength necessary to do anything in Jesus name—even move mountains.

Along with things that are *wrong* or *incorrect*, asking for things that are *unclear* or *confusing* are also things that are amiss. Double-mindedness is amiss. Double-mindedness is asking in a way that is unclear or confusing. It is any time your heart, mind, words, and actions conflict, causing confusion. Instead, we must learn to align our desires, thoughts, words, actions, and emotions, especially when praying for blessings from God. Our Father in heaven reads hearts and hears our words, but primarily he reads our hearts. This is how he communicates with us. If we have a conflict between our emotions and words, for example, our prayers may not be answered because of the conflict and confusion that it causes.

Asking for a needed blessing but feeling afraid not to ask causes confusion because God hears our words and reads our hearts. We may be so afraid to ask God for a blessing that we straddle between the wanting and needing of it and whatever feelings we have about asking for it. This is double-mindedness and asking amiss. Asking for two opposing things, even if the opposition is only in our minds and emotions, create a dichotomy between the concerns in the heart and the words used to request it. It goes against our agency so God cannot answer the prayer.

What would happen if you went into your local convenience store and asked for a product, repeatedly begging for the product but never saying exactly what you wanted; wincing, ducking, walking in and out of the store, hiding and gaining courage to speak, saying, "but no, I really do not want it because I feel guilty about taking it from you and I'm not worthy of it anyway, but I really need it so may I have one of those, but I am not sure if you will really give it to me, but I really want it and need it really badly. Please, please, pleeeeeease will you give it to me, but I know that you will not give it to me because I am not worthy of it. I know that I should not even ask for this because you have not told me that I could ask for it, but if you let me buy it this one time, I promise I will be a better person. I'll go to church every week and I will quit sinning, and I will never ask anything from you ever again?" The clerk would give you a strange look and possibly ask you to leave the store (perhaps even throwing things at you). Do you think you would be sold the product? Probably not.

If you were to vocalize all of the thoughts and emotions that you feel when you kneel to pray, would your prayers sound like this example? This is the biggest reason you do not receive the blessings you request—double-mindedness and amiss. God cannot answer this type of prayer because it is confusing, unclear, incorrect (it is incorrect to pray in this way), not really asking whether you want it or not. God's hands are tied and he cannot bless you.

Early in my life, I would ask for a blessing from God and was so afraid to ask that I would also ask not to have it. I would ask for the blessing and then say that I know that I am not worthy of it, so I know that he would not bless me, ending by begging for the blessing. I thought I was being humble in my request by asking in this way. God could not bless me because of my double-mindedness, just like the example above.

While this is the main type of double-mindedness, being a Sabbath Christian is another type. Going to church, putting forth an outward appearance for the rest of the congregation, and lying, cheating, and doing all types of other sins the rest of the week is double-mindedness. It's hypocrisy. God cannot cause a contradiction. God cannot bless you because of your sins. Sinning, even if it is part time, is sinning and God cannot look upon sin with any consent, so blessings would not be given due to double-mindedness (plus he reads what is in your heart).

> "If any of you lack wisdom, let him ask of God, that giveth to all men liberally, and upbraideth not; and it shall be given him. But let him ask in faith, nothing wavering, For he that wavereth is like a wave of the sea driven with the wind and tossed. For let not that man think that he shall receive any thing of the Lord; A double minded man is unstable in all his ways." (James 1:5–8 KJV)

How do you feel about these verses? Do you personally believe that if you want to know something, you can ask God and he will give it to you gladly and generously? Is it difficult to accept because the remaining verses cause some understanding with the language? Let us bring them down to their simplest meanings, to gain clarity:

'If you are confused about something, ask God who gives gladly and generously to all, and will not condemn you for asking, but you shall be given it. But be warned; let him ask in faith, nothing wavering, for he who wavers is like the waves of the sea, going back and forth. For anyone who wavers cannot think that he shall receive anything because anyone who straddles between two desires is unstable and does not ask of anything really.'

The last verse is a bit startling, is not it? When defining

double-mindedness, it is just like my example of going into a convenience store and asking for a product and, in the same breath, talking you out of asking for it. This verse talks about this exact thing.

When you request blessings from God, do your words waver like the waves of the sea, being tossed back and forth? Can you see the same wavering between your words and your emotions? Between your words and your actions? Perhaps bringing clarity to this verse helps you to understand why many of your prayers are unanswered. These verses do not tell us not to ask, but instruct us *how* to ask, giving warnings about what we could be doing wrong if we have asked for blessings from God and received nothing.

If your request is amiss, meaning that it is *wrong, confusing, unclear, or incorrect*, or you have double-mindedness, you have tied God's hands against you. He cannot do anything for you in any way because your words, emotions, and actions demonstrate your agency. But that means that if you have addressed all of them, you may request and receive your righteous desires.

There is another way to stop positive consequences and blessings through our agency, which you should understand. When emotion (an energy) is focused on (an energy) so that you receive an emotional reward (which is yet another energy) you may automatically stop positive consequences and blessings that you would otherwise receive because you have chosen to focus on that personal triple negative reward. These personal triple negative rewards are things like self-pity, complaining, gossip, negative attitude, judgment, lying, unforgiveness, manipulation, insidiousness, refusal to accept truths, and others. These activities have their own rewards and so those rewards are chosen rather than to receive requested blessings from God. Desiring these types of rewards can be seen as another type of double-mindedness, because seeking negative rewards were sought, using your agency.

On a real level, agency rules our lives. All experiences are results of our own or someone else's agency. Through it, we dictate whether we are a blessing or a curse to those around us. Even when we have to endure another person's choices, how we endure it and how we react to it is the result of our own agency. Through it, we dictate the extent to which God is able to bless our lives.

While many dread reading that last sentence, thinking of it negatively, if you flip it to the other side you may feel empowered. We are responsible for the negative and positive consequences of our own actions. This means that there are no universal forces working against us. Instead, we are able to consciously set up our lives so that we automatically receive more positive and less negative consequences by obeying the conditions of what God can or cannot do.

How do we do this? This is the direction we are facing on life's path, how we treat other people (compassion, forgiveness, etc.), and doing things in a way so God can bless us. As the God of the universe, if we face the Savior and try to move toward him, we are already positioned to receive favor and blessings from him. This sets up our lives to automatically receive more blessings due to our willingness (not our perfection) to be faithful and obedient to the laws that would bring us positive consequences. Once we have set our lives up so that we may receive more positive consequences and less negative ones, the most powerful way to receive more blessings is by asking for our righteous desires.

Since you know that an evil desire is anything that causes someone a loss so that you may win, asks for a sign, is against the law, would harm someone, would force someone to deny Jesus, would take someone's agency away, and anything of these done to a child, a righteous desire is everything else. Righteous desires are legal, ethical, and filled with equity; it must be good for all involved—a win/win situation—and it must support everyone's choice, agency, and free will, not forcing one's will on anyone in any way.

To refuse to ask is to willfully refuse to humble yourself to the point of asking for that which you need and desire. Many people, like I did, believe that we should not ask for things from God, and that by doing so would cause soul-losing consequences. Yet the Bible urges all to ask so that they may receive. What are we going to believe—man or God? Those teachings or beliefs are wrong. Even clearer, any teaching and belief that tells you not to ask God, is Satan's doings so that we are frustrated and confused about Jesus. In truth, God wants us to receive because all things either detract from or attract faith in Jesus. Receiving requested blessings glorifies Jesus and brings people to him. That means that the only thing holding you back from receiving blessings from God is that you do not ask.

> "Verily, verily, I say unto you, Whatsoever ye shall ask the Father in my name, he will give it you. Hitherto have ye asked nothing in my name: ask, and ye shall receive, that your joy may be full." (John 16:23–24 NKJV, italics added.)

These verses in John make it clear:

> "If ye abide in me, and my word abide in you, ye shall ask what ye will, and it shall be done unto you. Herein is my Father glorified that ye bear much fruit; so shall ye be my disciples." (John 15:7–8 KJV)

If your heart is Jesus' and if you are facing Christ on life's path, you will ask (an act of agency) whatever you will (also an act of agency) and it shall absolutely be done. To ask so that it shall be done is how the Father is glorified because it causes you to do much good in Jesus' name. Asking so that it can be received is a type of worship, because it glorifies the Father and the Son.

As we begin the next chapter, let your imagination roam. Do you have a dream that you have thought about for years? If it is not an evil desire, it is a righteous one. What about a college education for your children? That is a righteous desire. An ethic business is one. Your dream home is also one. Do you want to travel and see exotic destinations? That is a righteous desire. If it is not an evil desire, it is a righteous one. Do you have a blessing that you would like God to give to you? Think about how it would feel to receive it. All righteous desires are available to you from your Father in heaven by asking.

7

ASK AND YE SHALL RECEIVE

> **"Whatsoever ye shall ask in my name, that will I
> do, that the Father may be glorified in the Son. If ye
> shall ask any thing in my name, I will do it."**
> **(John 14:13–14)**

To create the relationship necessary to develop life-changing faith, we need to have good communication on both sides. Any relationship requires it. Good communication creates a close and trusting relationship, and communication with our Father in heaven and Savior is required—but we need to learn how to do it correctly so that we can receive the blessings for which we ask. In the last chapter, 'The Power to Choose Righteous Desires,' we learned that the most common error when asking for blessings from our Father in heaven is that we ask in ways that he is unable to answer—we tie his hands. We learned the various ways that we tie his hands against us. Unless we understand how to correct our errors, we will never gain the results we want and need, no matter how we try.

It is essential that we understand the truth about prayer, choose to change our beliefs about asking for and receiving blessings from God, and then learn how to ask for blessings in the correct way—in a way that God is able to answer. These few misconceptions about prayer can be easily swept away once Bible instructions are pointed out and understood.

When you ask God for a particular blessing, what types of things do you ask for? How often do you ask for blessings or help? What do you feel when you talk to him in prayer? What are your results? Do you only ask for large things that you are not able to do for yourself? Do you ever ask for simple things, like to know where you have placed your keys? Are there things for which you would never ask? What words do you use?

The Bible instructs us to pray. It tells us to hold a constant prayer in our hearts (Luke 18:1 KJV, 1 Thessalonians 5:17 KJV). We are to pray over all things, over our families, our flocks, and crops (currently, we are to pray about our jobs, our incomes, our houses, our cars, and our food) (Genesis 20:7 KJV, Genesis 25: 22 KJV). We are to pray for our brothers and sisters in the gospel (Ephesians 6:18 KJV). We are to pray to get closer to God and feel more of his Spirit (1 Thessalonians 5:18 KJV, Philippians 4:6 KJV, Ephesians 5:20 KJV). We are to give thanks to God for all he has done for us (Daniel 6:10 KJV, Philippians 4:6 KJV). We are to call on the Lord to be delivered from harm (Joel 2:32 KJV, 2 Chronicles 15:4 KJV). We are to pray for our enemies that their hearts will be softened toward us (Luke 6:28 KJV). We are to pray for forgiveness, so that our souls remain spotless and we are protected from temptation (2 Chronicles 7:14 KJV, 1 Thessalonians 5:23 KJV). We are to pray and watch for the Second Coming of Christ (Luke 21:36 KJV). We are to pray for blessings (Mark 11:24 KJV, Matthew 21:22-24 KJV, Philippians 4:6–8). We are to pray about all parts of our lives.

There is nothing too important or too scary about which we cannot talk to God. Likewise, there is nothing too minor or too unimportant about which we cannot talk to him, either. All things contribute to or take away our faith in Jesus, so all things that are important to us are also important to God. This life is not segregated into two different sections, those things that are spiritual and those that are temporal. All things contribute to our experiences, perceptions, and beliefs, and therefore, all things lead us to the decisions we make regarding the direction we face on life's path. All things influence our belief in Jesus.

People who are hungry, for example, may have difficulty gaining faith because they notice the needs of the flesh before anything else—the growling of hunger in the belly overpowers the whispers of the Spirit in the mind and heart. God understands this and the devil counts on it. Faith in the Savior may not even be on their radar because their empty stomachs and fatigue would drown most of what the Spirit whispers, especially if they had not had previous experience with the Spirit. In this life, our basic temporal needs may need to be met before we can understand God.

Prayer and sacrifice were given to man soon after Adam and Eve were sent out of the Garden of Eden. In the garden, Adam and Eve communed with God regularly. In their perfect and innocent state they walked with him and spoke with him face to face. Sin drove them from the garden where they were no longer able to commune with him as they had before, so prayer had to answer the need of people to commune with God, and sacrifice answered the need of justice so that God could listen and answer them, for God could not do so while they were guilty of sin.

Prayer is for us to connect with God, but prayer must be done correctly. In Matthew, Jesus warns us about a couple of incorrect ways to pray.

> "And when thou prayest, thou shalt not be as the hypocrites are: for they love to pray standing in the synagogues and in the corners of the streets, that they may be seen of men. Verily I say unto you, they have their reward. But thou, when thou prayest, enter into thy closet, and when thou hast shut thy door, pray to thy Father which is in secret; and thy Father which seeth in secret shall reward thee openly. But when ye pray, use not vain repetitions, as the heathen do: for they think that they shall be heard for their much speaking. Be not ye therefore like unto them: for your Father knoweth what things ye have need of, before ye ask him." (Matthew 6:5–8 KJV)

In these verses, Jesus corrects the Pharisees (orthodox blue-collar Jewish priests) and Sadducees (liberal Palestinian aristocratic priests) who argued about basic philosophy. The Pharisees and Sadducees fought about everything. The Pharisees were working priests who believed in the written and oral law, and believed that there was life after this one; where the Sadducees were wealthy priests, living in luxurious homes, which believed in only written law and believed that there was no life after this one. Subsequently, the two groups fought by preaching and praying for the others' errors, and debated on street corners (I can only imagine that the common people were very confused).

We see similar examples in our day between various leaders in differing denominations who argue about theology rather than understanding that people need different paths to Jesus. Specifically about prayer in our day, we can see that there are three types of prayers, those that I call mini sermon prayers, jargon prayers, and glory prayers (although I am sure that there may be others). Mini sermon prayers are typically prayers that either preview or summarize the topic said in the sermon, adding their personal interpretations, understandings, and knowledge—basically giving a mini sermon in their prayers. The preacher has done a good job preparing and giving their sermons, so to preview the sermon in the invocation (the prayer to invite the Spirit at the beginning of a meeting) or continue to preach in benediction (the prayer to close the meeting) is disrespectful and discredits the preacher. This long-winded prayer adds quoted scriptural references and uses other spiritual authorities to add to the mini sermon.

Jargon prayers are also long-winded prayers that use clichés, spiritual jargon, repetitive or memorized scriptural verses, and seem to preach to God, telling him what is happening as though he does not know. They use eloquent-sounding words and phrases to elevate their own worth, and may even correct the preacher in their prayers.

Glory prayers are those that are done either verbally or silently, usually done by symbols or other physical actions to show other people that they are praying, are spiritual, and God approves and blesses them inequitably. We see these types of prayers in restaurants, football end zones, on television situation comedies (sitcoms), and other public places. These types of prayers (and other types that use prayer for their own uses and rewards) are hypocritical and prideful, and should be avoided.

These types of prayers are not intended for God, but for the people who witness them, to make the person praying appear spiritual, intelligent, learned, and biblically versed (even if only in their own minds), and Jesus said that "they have their own reward." Instead, Jesus instructs us to pray secretly, in our closets (not seen by anyone), say humbly-worded prayers (not taking away from any part of the Spirit that may be at the meeting), and feeling the earnestness in our hearts (not memorized or dead words). We are to use words that illustrate our honest humility and respect, said in the heart and intended only for God. These types of prayers are those that make it to heaven and to God's ears.

> "After this manner therefore pray ye: Our Father which art in heaven, Hallowed be thy name. Thy kingdom come, Thy will be done in earth, as it is in heaven. Give us this day our daily bread. And forgive us our debts, as we forgive our debtors. And lead us not into temptation, but deliver us from evil: For thine is the kingdom, and the power, and the glory, for ever. Amen." (Matthew 6:9–13 KJV)

The Lord's Prayer patterns the spirit and content that should be said in our prayers. Again, this prayer was not intended to be a memorized prayer. Instead, this is a pattern for our prayers.

Most of us learned to pray as children. I do not presume to tell you how to pray, however there may be some misconceptions about the process of praying that may cause you to forfeit blessings from heaven (as it was for me), so it is essential that we touch on this very important prayer. The Bible records the process of praying by our Savior. Jesus gave us the prime example of how to pray in The Lord's Prayer. We understand that to pray correctly, we:

- **Address God.** You are addressing someone who is most important to you, so you want to always address your Father in heaven humbly and with respect. That being said, you also want to address him in a way that you can be vulnerable, let your guard down, and open up to him completely (if you cannot do this now, you will be able to as you continue your journey developing life-changing faith). Do it in a way that you feel that he is your father who loves you so much and wants to connect with you, as his child or a loved, trusted, and long-time friend or mentor.

- **Worship God.** To worship your Father in heaven, share your love, respect, devotion, adoration, and appreciation for the God of heaven and Earth. This may be the feelings that you experience as you bow yourself to your God, or you may vocally express your heartfelt devotion (or any other way that you worship God).

- **Thank God.** Thank God for all the blessings that he has given to you, acknowledging his great goodness shown toward you.

- **Ask for your desire.** Ensure that you think about the things that you are requesting from God. This takes some forethought and effort. Ensure that you ask in a way that he can answer and give you that which you request (we will learn how to do this next), submitting your will to his perfect will, understanding that he is all wise and, compared to him, you know nothing.

- **Ask for forgiveness.** God is not able to bless you when you are guilty of unrepented sins and so if you do not repent, for whatever reason, even forgetfulness, God cannot answer your prayers. It is essential to ask for forgiveness for sins committed so that you may retain God's love and favor toward you, and bring pleasure to him and his Son. It is always good to repent for specific sins, but because our nature is sinful and we will not be able to become perfect in this life, it is good to ask for forgiveness generally and for things that we may not remember. Repent now. Do not delay.

- **Ask for protection against and strength to resist temptation,** so that you may further the kingdom of God on Earth, and for the glory of our Father in heaven and Jesus.

- **Do all things in the name of Jesus Christ** by either beginning or ending your prayer. Because we have taken on ourselves the name of Jesus, we are to do all things in his name. The word *amen* is only necessary if you are praying with other people. The word *amen* is a request for all others hearing the prayer to reply in agreement, as if they were saying the prayer too (if you say the word *amen* earnestly and feeling the emotion of devotion or worship, even though someone else is saying the prayer, God accepts the prayer as if you spoke it yourself. If it is a group of people who agree to the prayer, by saying the word *amen*, and if they feel the heart-felt emotions of the prayer, God hears the pleas of each person individually and collectively. This is the power of prayer circles). If your prayer is a private conversation between you and your Father in heaven, saying the word *amen* is unnecessary.

Now that we have addressed hypocritical prayers and the correct basic content of our prayers, we need to learn how to pray in a way that God can answer you. There is a verse that talks about the power of an "effectual fervent prayer." This verse instructs us how to pray, giving us a clue how to correct that which we must do to gain the results of our prayers.

"The effectual fervent prayer of a righteous man availeth much." (James 5:16 KJV)

An "effectual fervent prayer" is more than an effective prayer. That term, "effectual fervent prayer" holds huge meaning, once understood. First, the prayer must be effectual. The definition *effectual* is something that is intended to produce success. For a prayer to be effectual it needs to be constructed specifically, clearly, and effectively, ensuring that there is no double-mindedness or anything that is amiss. Second, the prayer must also be fervent. The definition of *fervent* is a display of passion or intensity. To be fervent it must need to be powerful, and needs to hold heartfelt emotion. So, the *effectual fervent prayer* must be an efficiently devised prayer that is powerfully said in a way that your determination and devotion are felt. This is key.

Emotion is one of the missing ingredients in many prayers. Without the felt emotions in a prayer, it is lifeless and would hold no meaning (Matthew 6:7 KJV). It is the reason some prayers are not answered—God does not even receive them.

Have you watched and listened to a toddler pray? They hold their eyes and hands tightly as they intently say the things that are in their hearts and minds, leaving nothing out. Their little bodies are about to burst with excitement and intent as they explain things that they have learned or experienced that day, or ask for things that they are sure they will receive. This is an effectual fervent prayer, and this is why little children will lead us.

When you pray, you must engage your heart. Engaging the heart, really feeling the intent of your prayers, will be heard in the ears and heart of God far more than dead words. Remember that God communicates with us through our hearts primarily, and in our thoughts secondarily, so it makes sense that God receives our prayers through our hearts and then he can hear our words. The intent in your heart is the actual connection between you and Jesus. Our heart-felt emotion is what connects our faith to Jesus' power, which in turn is the bridge between us and the Father. Thinking about the words that you want to convey and feeling the earnestness in your heart ensures that God will hear you.

For years, I did not know how to pray with any substance. I really wanted blessings for my parents and my siblings, and the leaders of the country, and for the church leaders, but I prayed with no intent. I repeated nearly the same words each time and I wondered why I did not feel anything, and I did not receive answers to my prayers. I was so frustrated, and I would pray to learn the secrets to use my faith, which was also not answered. My prayers were not even getting out of the room. Then when I became complacent, which was in my nature to do from time to time, my prayers seem redundant. They were nothing more than hot air.

The Bible explains what God thinks about saying these types of prayers:

> "I will search Jerusalem with candles, and punish the men that are settled on their lees: that say in their heart, The Lord will not do good, neither will he do evil." (Zephaniah 1:12 KJV) (the *lees* is the bitter sediment of wine in a barrel, and is considered to be the most worthless part of something, talking about stagnancy in spirit)

"Ye are the salt of the earth: but if the salt have lost his savor, wherewith shall it be salted? it is thenceforth good for nothing, but to be cast out, and to be trodden underfoot of men." (Matthew 5:13 KJV)

This means that if we do not put any earnestness, any intent, any heartfelt emotion into our hearts, when we pray, our prayers are as useless as the sediment in a wine barrel and God will not do anything for us, bad or good (probably because he did not even receive our prayers). Likewise, salt that has lost its ability to make things taste better is also good for nothing and it is cast out. These verses show that God will not do anything for us if we become complacent for very long or if we pray without engaging our hearts. Revelation says it even clearer:

"I know thy works, that thou art neither cold nor hot: I would thou wert cold or hot. So then because thou art lukewarm, and neither cold nor hot, I will spue thee out of my mouth." (Revelation 3:15–16 KJV)

Most of the time, complacent prayers come from times of ease, but they may also come from feelings of unworthiness. Guilt can make us feel ashamed to bow before our God because of the sins we have committed (either unrepented sins, or previously forgiven sins but those about which we still feel guilty), so we stop praying altogether. If these are the causes of our complacent prayers, repentance is the only option.

Yet, we need to understand that complacent prayers are still prayers, even when they fall flat. There is no power to these prayers because there is no intent in our hearts and God does not receive them. While these prayers do not communicate to God, we still bow before our Maker, which does something very important for us.

The act of praying, of bowing before our God, is an act of agency that keeps us pointed toward Christ, even if we are not actively moving forward. While these are not optimal prayers, do not discount them. They are important place keepers on your path. When you stop praying that is when a spiritual sinkhole opens up and you find yourself on the slippery slope to hell, committing sins that you may not have otherwise committed (this is another lesson I learned the hard way).

Complacent prayers may not hold the power of intended prayers but they can keep you safe for a short time until you re-engage your heart. Times of complacency are normal on our spiritual quest. These are times when we may need to take a break, sit under a tree, and rest for a while. As you begin your spiritual education, you may become overwhelmed. You need that time to take it all in, to let it soak into your soul and your understanding. These times of complacency may simply be a time to get re-grounded and to regain your spiritual footing before moving forward in your schooling with the Spirit.

Complacency may also be the beginning of the end, if allowed to continue. You can sit under a tree, fall asleep, and remain so unless you intentionally wake, open your Bible, and put your heart back into your prayers. The best way I have found to do this is to express your deep gratitude and love for your Father in heaven and his Son, and reaffirm the surrender of your will to them. You cannot complacently surrender your will to your Father and Savior, and praise his name. It just does not work.

The verses above, in Revelation, states that God would rather that we be cold or hot, not lukewarm (complacent). He would rather us be passionate toward God or rebellious against him because at least we have chosen a side. Straddling between righteousness and evil is never a good idea. God not only does not like that and will spue you out of his mouth. If our complacency continues, our faith dies.

> "And Elijah came unto all the people, and said, How long halt ye between two opinions? If the Lord be God, follow him: but if Baal, then follow him." (1 Kings 18:21 KJV)

Just as Elijah asked, 'How long will you sit between two beliefs? If you are for Jesus, follow him; but if you are for Satan, then follow him,' being complacent too long in our spiritual lives is just like being complacent in your job, your marriage, or anything else. If you are complacent in your job, for example, you are not really working, and you will soon lose it. It is the same with your relationship with our Father in heaven and Jesus. If you are complacent too long, you will lose the connection with them, and will eventually lose the understanding that they have given you (the spiritual sinkhole).

One of the most important things that I have learned about spiritual complacency is that if we do not receive blessings, for whatever reason (even including not asking for them), we lose our fervor, become complacent, and our faith dies. Faith needs the regular nutrients and fuel of received blessings (even miracles) for our faith to grow and blossom. We need to feel the awe and amazement when we receive blessings from God. That means that our hearts need to be engaged, really feel something, when we pray, so that we know that God receives them (know that I am not talking about fanaticism. I am talking about feeling love, devotion, or worship. We are still expected to experience this earthly life.

We are not to be lukewarm, but should have a burning, passionate flame in our spirits. The best way to prevent complacency is to ask for and receive all sorts of blessings, especially miracles (miracles cannot produce faith but it can intensify it). We cannot be complacent while receiving blessings from God and feel the awe, humility, and gratitude that always follows.

In the chapter, 'The Power to Choose Righteous Desires,' we learned the types of things for which we may pray and the types of things for which we should not pray. We learned that we are able to pray for all kinds of righteous desires, and we can easily see if our desires are righteous by seeing that they are not evil ones. Agency is so important to God that Satan is prevented from taking it when he tempts us. God cannot take someone's agency away, and so we should ensure that we do not request things that take agency away—ours as well as anyone else's. We learned about things that are amiss, things that cause double-mindedness, and those things that will tie God's hands against us so that he is unable to answer. So, thinking about how to pray in a way that God can answer us, we must ensure that we do not do these things. These must be our primary considerations.

"Moreover as for me, God forbid that I should sin against the Lord in ceasing to pray for you: but *I will teach you the good and right way.*" (1 Samuel 12:23 KJV, italics added)

Ensuring that we intend to pray for a righteous desire, we must first and always keep agency in the foreground of our minds when constructing our requests for blessings, in our prayers.

Many times we go to our Father in prayer and ask for his help— "help me" or "help my child." We request a healing with the words, "heal me." Other times, we kneel and talk to God, using the things that come to mind, as we kneel. We do not use any prior thought about what we want to say in our prayers, saying the first thing that comes to our minds. We are so desperate for the blessings that we end up begging for it, spewing nothing more than words and raw emotions, feeling the fear in our hearts and causing double-mindedness. God cannot answer these prayers. To request blessings in this way, we cannot expect to be given. It is far too vague and confusing for God to answer, *because of our agency.*

Instead, take the time to think about exactly what it is that you desire—before you kneel to pray. While we are able to thank God for blessings that he has given us without much forethought, expressing our heartfelt emotions, we need to carefully devise a request for blessings beforehand. We are to *construct* a request, not just throw it together.

When we request blessings, we must be clear and very specific (do you remember the definition of *amiss?* Amiss is anything that is *wrong, incorrect, unclear,* or *confusing).* If we construct our request for blessings *effectually,* we will ensure that it is *not wrong, incorrect, unclear,* or *confusing.* We must devise a prayer for that which is righteous (not wrong), it must ensure that everyone's agency is intact (not incorrect), it must be very specific (not unclear), and must ensure that we address our double-mindedness (not confusing). Then, if we make the request, ensuring that our hearts are engaged (*fervent*), our Father in heaven will receive our prayer, and will be able to answer and give us that which we desire. When we ask very specifically and we receive the blessing, just as we asked, we know that it is by God's hand that we received. This knowledge strengthens our faith in a way that no other way can, and this is the only reason for God to give us blessings—to strengthen our faith in Jesus. This is key.

Think about a blessing you want. Think about your desire. If it is an illness, do you have any idea what it is or what may have caused it? Find some possibilities. Do a little research. Talk to someone who may have an idea, or see a doctor. Then, word your request very specifically, explaining exactly what you want, as if you were required to design the blessing verbally. Exactly what result do you want? If you had the power to bless yourself, what exact results do you want? Explain in the tiniest detail. What would it look like and feel like? Asking these questions helps you to clarify, in your mind, what you desire before presenting it to the Father, in prayer. Look and see what else you may experience that may cause additional problems, if the blessing was given exactly as you request. Thinking about additional issues that may arise gives you the opportunity to include the entire process in your initial request.

Every time my small granddaughter would come to visit, she would pull her pierced earrings, with locking backs, out of her ears and would lose them (I still cannot figure out how she got the backs unlocked without tearing her earlobes). I knew that God knew exactly where the earrings were and I wanted to see them. Thinking about it, I did not want to ruin the tiny gold pieces by stepping on them or stabbing them into my feet, so I did not want to *find* them. I also did not want my granddaughter to swallow them, possibly finding them later in her diaper or have the doctor find them in the emergency room. I thought about how I wanted to find the earrings and constructed my request specifically, so I knew exactly what I wanted God to do for me. I wanted help to see them, and the backs, and I wanted her to be protected from swallowing them. So, I ask God to prevent my granddaughter from picking up the earrings and the backs and putting them into her mouth, and asked him to help me to *see* her earrings *and the backs*. This is a very specific request. God guided me to see the glint of light on all four tiny gold pieces, outside of her crib in the carpet, as I came into the room to put her down to sleep. They were in different places, but I saw the sparkle of the gold, like glitter, on the floor, telling me that it was God blessing me with that request.

Another time I had a skin infection on my arm and down onto my hand, during a time when I had no medical insurance. My skin was very sore, burning, and very itchy. Thinking it through, I realized that I did not know exactly what it was and could not even guess the cause of the infection. To cover all bases, I looked for possibilities on the internet, finding photographs of infections that looked similar to mine. There were several. I learned that my infection could have been caused by yeast, bacterium, toxin, or parasite (great!). I presented my case to my God in prayer. I explained that I did not know what it was for sure, but asked that he "kill the yeast, bacteria, toxins, parasites, or whatever may have caused the infection," which was a very specific request. The next morning I woke to find that I received my blessing exactly as I had requested. The problem was that the area was so sore, and itched far worse than it ever did before because the infection had been killed, but several layers of damaged skin was still inflamed and was not healed.

I realized that while I specifically requested to kill the infection, I did not request a desired outcome. Feeling kind of silly, I went back to God and asked him to "comfort, soothe, and heal the skin through all layers." This blessing was granted and the next morning I woke with just minor itching as the top layers of skin needed to slough off. The inflammation and soreness in the tissue was gone. I suffered an extra day because I did not think it through.

In the Bible, we see examples of very specific prayers. Recorded healings in the New Testament were specific requests: Give me my sight, heal my leprosy, help me walk, raise my daughter. The very best scriptural example of a specific prayer is found in Genesis. Abraham sent his servant to find a wife for his son, Isaac. Abraham instructed his servant to go to Abraham's family's region. When he arrived, he prayed to God regarding the woman he had in mind for a wife for Isaac. He asked God in a very specific manner to show him his will:

> "O Lord God of my master Abraham, I pray thee, send me good speed this day, and shew kindness unto my master Abraham. Behold, I stand here by the well of water; and the daughters of the men of the city come out to draw water; and *let it come to pass that the damsel to whom I shall say, Let down thy pitcher, I pray thee, that*

*I may drink; and she shall say, Drink, and I will give thy
camels drink also; let the same be she that thou hast appointed
for thy servant Isaac and thereby shall I know that thou hast
shewed kindness unto my master.*" (Genesis 24:12–14 KJV,
italics added)

First the servant presented his proposal and explained what he was
doing: he was standing at the well watching the young maids of the
city come out to get water. He would have probably felt overwhelmed
to see how many there were and would not know which one to choose.
He asked his request very specifically: 'Let the woman who is chosen
as Isaac's wife that I would ask her for a drink, and so I know for sure
that it is her, let her say that she will give water to my camels also.' This
is a very specific request. Note that his request was so specific that he
asked God to even lead him to ask for a drink from the chosen woman.
"Let it come to pass that the damsel to whom *I shall say....*" He probably
planned on asking all of the women at the well and then waited for the
correct response, but God took his words literally (which he will) and
pushed him to ask for a drink of Rebekah, which was the woman God
had chosen. He surrendered his will to God and requested in a way that
God can answer and he, as a fallible human, cannot mistakenly choose
the wrong one.

Later that evening, as he recounted, to Rebekah's family, all that
had happened, he told them how quickly God had answered his prayer:

"And *before I had done speaking* in mine heart, behold,
Rebekah came forth with her pitcher on her shoulder;
and she went down unto the well, and drew water: and I
said unto her, Let me drink, I pray thee." (Genesis 24:45
KJV, italics added)

Of course, this servant did as many of us do when God answers our
prayer in the manner requested, he wondered if this was really an answer
from God:

"And the man, wondering at her, held his peace, to wit whether God had made his journey prosperous or not." (Genesis 24:21 KJV)

It is often startling when God answers our prayers, especially in the beginning. We are humbled and left in awe by his tender mercies, like Abraham's servant felt. He kept quiet and wondered whether God really had blessed him, mainly because of the quickness of the answer. But when Rebekah told him that she was from Abraham's brother's house, he felt that humbling feeling of knowing that his prayer had been answered:

"And the man bowed down his head, and worshiped God, and he said, Blessed be God of my master Abraham, who hath not left destitute my master of his mercy and his truth; I being in the way, God led me to the house of my master's brethren." (Genesis 24:26-27 KJV)

This beautiful account of faith illustrates all points of using life-changing faith to request and receive blessings. The servant detailed what both people would do to attest that this is the woman whom God had chosen for Isaac. This is not asking for a sign. A sign has to do with receiving an answer that had not been asked. This is a confirmation from God that his prayer had been answered. Abraham's servant surrendered his will to God and only asked to be shown God's will in a way that he would unmistakably recognize. Also, his wondering if God had answered his prayer was not doubt or lack of faith, but it was the humbling awe and amazement when humans feel the touch of deity in that perfect moment. Our prayers need to be this specific—because of our agency.

I highly recommend that you write the words you intend to pray, as you construct your requested blessing, until you can construct it in your mind without missing any components (this is the first half of constructing your *prayer of faith*, which is a constructed *effectual fervent prayer*).

To construct a successful request, think about the blessing that you want:

1. **Is it a righteous desire?** Look to ensure that it is a righteous desire. In the chapter, 'The Power to Choose Righteous Desires,' we discussed that a righteous desire is anything that is not an evil one. We understand that it is far easier for us to see if our desires are righteous if we look to see that they are not evil, does not do anything against the law, does not entice anyone to sin, does not cause harm, does not cause someone to win while someone else loses, does not interfere with or remove someone's agency or choice in any way, does not do anything that takes anyone further away from Jesus, and does not do any of these things to a child or someone who is otherwise innocent. Have you considered what receiving this blessing may do for you and your family? Have you considered the possible positive and negative consequences of receiving this blessing? Once you have identified that your request is a righteous desire, go to the next step.

2. **Think deeply about exactly how you want to experience the blessing.** Think about things before presenting them to your Father in heaven in prayer so that you are able to construct the prayer very specifically, like Abraham's servant did. What have you done to obtain this desire and what results did you experience? If you had to verbally design your blessing, what exactly would you want and specifically how would you like to experience it? Remember that we discussed the need for our requests to be very specific or God may not be able to answer our prayers, because asking for things that are vague interferes with our agency. How do you want the blessing given to you so that you would know that it was an answer from God? If this blessing was received exactly as requested, are there any possible resulted issues that could occur (make sure that your results are as you want them)?

    Note that in the examples of people requesting healing blessings from Jesus, they asked him to do it. Many times we ask for *help* doing something. This will not produce the same results as asking for God to do it for you. We do not really want *help* doing something, for God has the power to do things that we cannot do for ourselves. So, word your request asking for God to do whatever it is that you want, from him, resisting the word *help* in your request.

Once you have pondered your desire, looking at it from all angles and know exactly how you want to receive it, move to the next step.

3. **Address anything that is amiss or causes double-mindedness.** What resistance, doubt, fear, anxiety, etc., do you feel regarding the thought of asking for this desire from God? Make it clear in your mind. Write it all down. Get it clear enough so you are able to explain it all. In the chapter, 'The Power to Choose Righteous Desires,' we discussed the possibility of double-mindedness and how this interferes with our petitions to the Father, asking for the blessing and asking not to receive the blessing in the same breath because our emotions may cancel our verbal request. Do you have any feelings of disbelief or distrust regarding asking for blessings from God? If all of your emotions and words would be said at the same time in your prayer to God, what would they say (because they will)? Once you have written all of your feelings, move to the next step.

4. **Write it all down.** If it is clearer for you to write your entire prayer, do so. God never said that you cannot read your prayers. Make sure that you put your heartfelt emotions into your words, however. If it is better for you to use a bullet point list, use that. Just make sure that you write the parts of your prayer that you are constructing, in the beginning, so that you make sure that it is correct, as you learn.

This is how clearly constructed our requests of blessings need to be, specifying exactly what we want our Father in heaven to do for us (the reason why I say that we need to *construct* a prayer rather than to *devise* one is because that there are different components that need to be put together to *build* an effectual fervent prayer [I call it a *Prayer of Faith*], even though grammatically *device* is correct. The visual of building, like building a structure, gives more understanding). Just as we cannot build a building in a day, we cannot construct an effectual fervent prayer in the seconds when we kneel to pray and start praying. We need to think through the strong emotions that we may feel at the time to think exactly what we want to request, communicating what we really mean and want. The clearer we can express our meaning and feelings in our words, the more powerful our communications will be; and the more clearly we express ourselves to our Father in heaven and our Savior, the more communications and blessings we will receive from them. This is key.

There is a spiritual tool that I invite you to use. This tool is very specific and is used to gain God's will for you and also shows just how specific you need to be in your requests with your Father in heaven—a *stupor*. I have mentioned stupors a couple of times through this book but I wanted to wait for this moment so that you received all of the information regarding them. A stupor is my favorite spiritual tool. They are amazingly powerful and relatively simple. They have blessed my life in so many ways and I know that when you try them, you will love them too.

A stupor is a tool that you can request to remove something from your mind, heart, and/or whole or part of your body, such as thoughts, emotions, and/or sensations or cravings, respectively. One of the definitions of a stupor is *oblivion*: a state of being unaware or something forgotten. This is exactly what a stupor does. It removes or makes something oblivious in the mind, heart, or body.

There are two basic purposes for using a stupor. Primarily, a stupor is a tool to show you God's will on a matter. Because we all have ideas (thoughts), feelings (emotions), and bodily sensations (sensations/cravings), you may use a stupor to learn God's will for you, by using them. Assessing what you experience, a thought, feeling, or sensation/craving, you are able to request a stupor of one or more of them in your mind, heart, or body, respectively, if it goes against God's will. If whatever you requested is removed, in that you no longer experience the feelings, emotions and/or sensations any longer, it shows you a clear indication that what you asked about goes against God's will for you, thus showing you clearly his will. I call this type a *wisdom stupor.*

Secondarily, you may request that experienced thoughts, emotions, or sensations be removed simply because they cause you discomfort. These types of things may be overwhelming temptation, obsessive thoughts or other types of thoughts, double-mindedness, anxiety or fear, cravings, emotions, or sensations. You may request a stupor to remove them from your mind, heart, and/or whole or part of your body so that they no longer bother you, using your agency. They can also be requested for other people, too, as an appeasement, forgetfulness, etc. I simply call these *oblivion stupors*.

The key to constructing a successful stupor is that the request must be specific so that you receive the answer in the clearest and most unmistakable way for you, like Abraham's servant's request. The more specific-yet-simple you can construct it, the more success you will have and the clearer your answer will be.

To construct a *wisdom stupor*, it is essential that you first assess where you experience the sensation: your mind, heart, and/or body. To assess things that are in your mind, you would think about thoughts, questions, temptation, attitudes, and all things that you think of. To assess things that are in your heart, you would feel any type of emotion, such as anxiety, fear, attraction, sadness, pressures from temptation, love, etc. To assess things in your body, take an inventory of what you are physically feeling, such as cravings, pain, twitches, cramps, burning sensations, cough, and all other types of physical sensations. For clarity, we will call them all *effects*.

Once you have assessed what you are experiencing in the three areas, mind, heart, and body, you simply list all of the effects that you experience. To ask for a stupor using all experienced effects in all of the three areas makes your answer clearer. To request a stupor in one area when it is experienced in two or all three areas can cause confusion.

The first time I used this tool, I requested a *wisdom stupor* in my mind only. I received the stupor in my mind, as I had requested, and the thought was no longer there (showing me that it was against God's will), but the feelings associated with the thought remained. I did not understand that I had some associated feelings with the thought until the thought was gone, which caused me confusion.

There are feelings associated with many of our ideas, so a *wisdom stupor* requested from both the mind and heart would offer clarity. Now I simply request a stupor of my mind and heart every time I use one, as default, to make sure that I receive the clearest answer possible, and then assess if there is a physical sensation with it.

Does this make that much of a difference, you may ask? It makes all the difference in the world. Say for instance that you are looking at a particular person as a possible mate and want to know God's will. If the person you ask God about goes against his will, requesting a *wisdom stupor* in your mind would remove the thought of that person as a good mate but would leave the feelings of attraction in your heart, thereby causing confusion. Clarity comes by asking for a stupor in *all* areas in which you experience them. Asking for both mind and heart, as default, covers both of them every time and then assess if you also experience anything in your body (nerves, cells, organs, etc.).

To request this *basic wisdom stupor*, you ask for God's will about your idea. You present your idea to him as you would detail a business proposal. Explain the idea, detailing what you are thinking and feeling about it (and bodily sensations, if applicable). Ask that if it go against God's will for you that he give you a stupor to your mind and heart (and body, if applicable) so that they no longer bother you. If it goes against God's will for you, you will receive a stupor and the idea will no longer hold any power, and may not be thought about again for some time, remembering it later as unimportant. If the idea is God's will for you, you will retain the idea and emotions as before.

While a *basic wisdom stupor* is powerful, I was thinking about Abraham's servant's prayer and how very specific it was. Pondering this, I came up with what I call a *double-edged wisdom stupor* that works even better than a basic one at seeing God's will, because the primary purpose of a *wisdom stupor* is to ensure that you know God's will for you in the clearest possible way. A *double-edged wisdom stupor* is even more powerful and is more specific in its request because it helps you to address the things that may cause you to question the information from the *basic wisdom stupor* (anxiety, fear, etc.), or may be used when you have more than one choice. There is a table below that has a numbered list of effects (i, ii, iii, etc.), and three components (1, 2a, 2b) to construct the *double-edged wisdom stupor*, making it easier to create. The numbering in the parentheses, in the next paragraph, references the components in the table.

To construct a *double-edged wisdom stupor*, you detail the matter, the idea, etc., and assess where you are experiencing it; your (i) mind, (ii) heart, (iii) body (if applicable), and (iv) understanding (if applicable). Then you ask God that (1) if whatever you are asking about is against God's will for you that he would remove it from your (i) mind, (ii) heart, (iii) body (if applicable), and (iv) understanding (if applicable) so that it does not bother you any longer (*basic wisdom stupor*); BUT that (2a) if it is his will for you that (a) it becomes bright and brilliant in your (i) mind, (ii) heart, (iii) body (if applicable), and (iv) understanding (if applicable), AND that (2b) all fear, doubt, confusion, [add what you feel would help you] and anything else that would keep you from moving forward with it be removed from your (i) mind, (ii) heart, (iii) body (if applicable), and (iv) understanding (if applicable) so that they do not bother you any longer. A *basic wisdom stupor* is all the step 1 instructions, and a *double-edged wisdom stupor* are the instructions in all three steps, 1, 2a, and 2b.

The *double-edged wisdom stupor* brings you the most unmistakable answer because it is more specific and empowers what you are experiencing, making them feel powerful, and addresses any fear, doubt, etc., that you may experience. Please note that you may add other things to the areas in which you experience your effects ([i] mind, [ii] heart, etc.), such as (v) gut instincts. I added (iv) understanding to the pattern but it can be removed because understanding and gut instincts can be considered part of the mind. If you feel that you need to separate them, add them but remember that simplicity is best. Using your thoughts and emotions to highlight and alleviate concerns or fears in the second stupor makes seeing God's will so much easier to decipher. If it is God's will to follow your idea, not only are you left with your own idea, plans, and excitement, but they are brightened and made more powerful; and your fears and concerns are addressed and removed.

This dual approach to a stupor is the clearest way to receive an answer about anything. It is extremely specific and removes one thing or the other from your mind and heart (and body, if applicable), clearly leaving you with our Father's will. After requesting a stupor, go about your normal activities. The stupor will tell you which way to proceed. I usually receive them overnight, knowing the answer when I awake the next morning, although I have also experienced instant stupors (usually *oblivion stupors*).

You can ask for *oblivion stupors* for many things. Anything that is in your mind, heart, or body, can be removed with a stupor. *Oblivion stupors* occur instantly because God sees that you need rescue in that moment (although I have realized that there is a short pause—a couple of seconds— between the time I have requested the stupor and the time it occurs. I wonder if it is a type of test of my faith). Basically, you use it like a *basic wisdom stupor*, explaining what you are experiencing and explain why you want it removed. You ask for the stupor of that effect in the place experienced (mind, heart, or body). Through an *oblivion stupor*, I have requested a rescue and removal of especially difficult temptation; from fear or anxiety; for dreams that Satan placed into my dreams, night after night; bronchial coughing fits that were exhausting and painful, sending electric shocks into my head and down my arms; nerve pain; worry for my children (you cannot stop being a mother); and many others. Instead of asking for the effects to be removed if it goes against God's will for you, however, you simply explain what you are experiencing and why you want them removed, asking to do so *using your agency*.

It is fascinating to completely forget something that was so brilliant in your mind and so strong in your emotions, and remember it later and wonder why you felt so strongly about it. It may creep back into your mind as a faded memory of something that you had forgotten, or you may feel a severe fading with regard to your request—something like it being moved to a far-away part of your mind and viewed as unimportant. The removal from your heart, however, is complete. The emotions are simply not there any longer. It is as if someone plucked them out. It may leave you wondering what on Earth you were thinking! The removal of the bodily sensation may be dissolved through time or immediate. I have experienced both but they were immediately lessened.

The easiest way to construct a *double-edged wisdom stupor* is with the following table:

Constructing a Stupor	1. Against God's Will	2a. God's Will	2b. God's Will
(i) Mind **(ii) Heart** **(iii) Body/Cells** (change this to the specific part of the body) Possibly adding (iv) Understanding and (v) Gut Instincts, if it adds more clarity, in your answer.	Request that God remove _____ _____ from your (i) (ii) (iii) [(iv) (v)] (strike all that do NOT apply), if it is against God's will, so that it does not bother you any longer.	BUT if it is God's will, it becomes brighter and brilliant in your (i) (ii) (iii) [(iv) (v)] (strike all that do NOT apply).	AND that all fear, doubt, confusion, _____ _____, and any other thought or emotion that would cause fear to move forward with it, be removed so that it does not bother you any longer and _____ _____.

The table above lists all of the components of constructing a *double-edged wisdom stupor*, as explained above. The first row across the table show the components, showing the *basic* (1) and *double-edged* (1, 2a, and 2b) *stupors* in the column headers in the top row; and your *effects* in your (i) mind, (ii) heart, (iii]) body or cells, (iv) understanding, and (v) gut instincts in the first column down the side.

Think about the *effects* in the different areas you experience them and cross off the areas that do NOT apply in the second column, 1. Against God's Will, creating the *basic wisdom stupor*. You will use the same *effects* in the *double-edged stupor*, so also cross the same areas that do not apply in the next column, 2a. God's Will. Understand that the point of creating a *double-edged wisdom stupor* is to receive an answer that is unmistakably clear, so that you understand God's will regarding the matter,without error (like the prayer of Abraham's servant), and so you will want to use what you already experience to find God's will for you, adding additional information in column 2b, if it would help you (2b helps to address anything that would cause you to NOT follow through with your idea, like fear, doubt, inability to succeed, etc.). My table would look like this:

Constructing a Stupor	1. Against God's Will	2a. God's Will	2b. God's Will
(i) **Mind** **(ii)** **Heart** **(iii)** **Body/Cells** (change this to the specific part of the body) Possibly adding (iv) Understanding and (v) Gut Instincts, if it adds more clarity, in your answer.	Request that God remove _Creating my XYZ Business_ from your (i) (ii) (⋈) [(⋈) (⋈)] (strike all that do NOT apply), if it is against God's will, so that it does not bother you any longer.	BUT if it is God's will, it becomes brighter and brilliant in your (i) (ii) (⋈) [(⋈) (⋈)] (strike all that do NOT apply).	AND that all fear, doubt, confusion, ———— ———— ————, and any other thought or emotion that would cause fear to move forward with it, be removed so that it does not bother you any longer and _and I feel confident in my decision_ .

In this example, I want to know if creating XYZ Business is God's will for me to do. In the first stupor column, 1. Against God's Will, I think about my business and where I experience it. In this case, I experience my thoughts (ideas, plans, and dreams) and emotions (excitement, anticipation, and fear). If it is against God's will for me to pursue the creation of my XYZ Business, I would like to receive the stupor in my mind and heart because I experience my thoughts and emotions, so I strike the other options (iii [body/cells], iv [understanding], and v [gut instincts]), in the table.

To make my *basic wisdom stupor* into a *double-edged wisdom stupor*, I think about what would help me as I pursue my venture to build my XYZ Business. In column, 2a. God's Will, I think about where I want to experience the stupor if this business is God's will for me to do. In this example, I want my thoughts and emotions to be brighter and more brilliant in my (i) mind and (ii) heart because if my thoughts, ideas, and excitement were to be made brighter and more brilliant, it would show me that I am on the right track and would help me be more successful creating it because God would have empowered them, making them brighter and more brilliant. In column 2b, I do not have additional concerns other than those that are already there: fear and doubt (which will be the main ones for most wisdom stupors), so I did not add additional ones. Then thinking about what would be helpful, if it is God's will for me, I thought that to feel confident in my decision would help me most, so I added this to the end of the text in column 2b, understanding that God can give me those feelings.

When you ask God for your stupor, follow your construction guide (the filled table). Pray, being open and genuine with God (if you are nervous, tell him. If you are experimenting with this information, tell him. Do not cause double-mindedness by trying to hide your fears or concerns. Instead counter any conflict that you are feeling, even if you do not notice them clearly enough, ask that God take your words over anything that you are feeling and thinking, using your agency). Ensure that you feel the deep feelings of desire and earnestness toward the blessing you request, to make sure that your heart is engaged. Do not merely say the words or this prayer will be dead words and God will not hear it.

Follow your construction guide, as you pray. This is what my prayer would sound like, following the stupor script, on the table, changing the pronouns appropriately (in brackets) and addressing the components of the stupor. You do not need to say the parenthetic information. This is only there so that you can accurately follow the components. Otherwise, simply follow the table. The single quotations will indicate the script information in the guide:

"My dear Father in heaven, in the name of Jesus Christ I come to you to ask your wisdom for me. I have been thinking and planning to create XYZ Business. I am very excited about it and have enough ideas and plans to think seriously about moving forward toward starting it, but I want your will in this matter. I know that I am fallible and you have all wisdom, so I really want your will, knowing that you see what is best for me and can see if this will be a good thing, in your perfect perspective. I ask that you give me a stupor if it goes against your will. I ask that you 'remove the ideas and feelings of creating my XYZ Business from my (i) mind and my (ii) heart if it is against [your] will, so that it no longer bothers [me]; BUT if it is [your] will they become brighter and brilliant in [my] (i) mind and (ii) heart; AND that all fear, doubt, confusion, and any other thoughts or emotions that would cause fear moving forward be removed so that it does not bother [me] any longer, blessing me with confidence about my decision....' " Continue your prayer as normal.

Stupors are very specific requests for God's will so that we receive his will in a way that we unmistakably recognize. Like with all other types of requests to God, ensure that your heart is engaged and that you are feeling the intent in your request.

Even though stupors are very powerful tools, there are some things that God cannot get past, but we can use our agency to counter them. Understanding that double-mindedness is anything where two parts of your life (thoughts and emotions, words and actions, etc.) conflict. God cannot get past them to give you blessings, because of your agency but you can use your agency to counter them.

Above, when explaining how to pray for a stupor, I addressed the possibility that you may be nervous praying about one. I suggested that you tell God about your nervousness, and ask that he take your words over anything that you were feeling and thinking, 'using your agency.' This is how you can counter your double-mindedness with your agency. You cannot use this, however, if your actions or behaviors are the things that cause the conflict, because it is your agency that causes it. You are not able to be blessed from God until you intentionally rectify the conflict by either stopping the action or changing the behavior. God cannot go against your agency. When praying, if you realize that your emotions conflict with your thoughts, feeling nervous about asking for a blessing, for example, you simply explain that you feel emotions that conflict with your words, but that you ask God to take your words over anything that you may be feeling or thinking, using your agency. Using your agency to counter any conflicting emotions puts weight on your words and asks God to disregard any conflicting thoughts and emotions. You can even add, "And anything else that may cause a conflict with my words". Just ensure that you explain that you are using your agency to do it. To say that you are *using your agency*, is the key.

There have been several times when I wanted to more closely follow my Savior but I knew that I also desired to re-experience the rewards of sin too. Praying and asking for a stupor to rid me of these desires created a problem because God and I both knew that I wanted to continue to re-experience the results of the sin. Struggling with the Spirit, I finally explained that I chose to use my agency to rid me of the desire for the sin, and asked that God take my words over anything that I felt, using my agency, so that I am released from the temptation.

I hope you are beginning to see just how specific we need to be in our requests to God. This is quite different from what we learned as children. I am sure that you also see that this is how the Bible instructs us to request blessings from him. To develop life-changing faith, all of our requests must be this clear because it honors our agency (actually, it *uses* it), and ensures that God is able to answer us every time we ask. As we finish the last few chapters, you will see how all of the tools work together to immediately help you gain the results that you desire, asking and receiving blessings from heaven.

8

RECOGNIZING THE
SPIRIT'S VOICE

"My sheep hear my voice, and I know them, and they follow me."
(John 10:27 KJV)

Recognizing the Spirit is the most important aspect of developing life-changing faith and is the most complicated part because of our human nature. It takes practice to recognize God's voice. As humans, we think first and then feel, for the most part. That means that we are doing things opposite of how God does it. While we communicate with words primarily (or exclusively), God communicates primarily with feelings in our hearts, and may use one or two words, or none at all.

As we learned in the last chapter, 'Ask and Ye Shall Receive,' prayer is vitally important to build a relationship with our Father in heaven and our Savior. The other side of communicating with our Father in heaven is the need to recognize and receive the messages and accurately decipher what they mean. We need to communicate with our Father in heaven and Savior much more than they need to communicate with us. The only way for us to obey God is if we are able to accurately listen so that we can recognize his voice and understand what he is telling us.

Recognizing the voice of the Spirit is a skill that must be learned. Recognizing the presence of Spirit (our Father in heaven, our Savior, and the Holy Spirit) and following the promptings given are vitally important to developing life-changing faith—it is the most important thing. At least, we need to learn to recognize the possibility that the Spirit could be sending a message.

As we create a relationship with God, we are taught truths and insights that we have not known before. We are taught "precept... upon precept, precept upon precept; line upon line, line upon line; here a little, and there a little" (Isaiah 28:10 KJV). This is how Deity teaches us. If we ignore or neglect to obey the promptings given, even if it is because we do not recognize them, the precept (or blessing) is lost to us; for we must do that which we are instructed to do to gain the full understanding that comes after we have obeyed. We must use a small amount of faith before we are taught the fullness of the lesson. Sometimes we are commanded to do something that is required before a blessing is given. So, if we ignore the Spirit or neglect his instructions, we would lose what we would otherwise have gained. If we ignore or neglect the promptings long enough, whether due to ignorance or willfulness, the Spirit may withdraw from us and cease sending messages. This is why it is important to remember Abraham's example. This is key.

Abraham seemed to be always vigilant. He was always anticipating messages from God, listening and answering immediately. He had learned to hone into God's *frequency,* and kept his heart and mind into that *channel*, always listening and feeling for messages. When he received a message, he answered immediately: "Here I am" (Genesis 22:1). Then he deciphered the messages accurately and immediately did what he was instructed to do, without questions, complaints, or wondering if it is his imagination. This is exactly what we need to learn to do, too. This is the goal. Like every new skill, it takes some effort, but it is not difficult. To keep an open channel of communication with God is like holding a prayer in our hearts.

Most of you, if not all, have experienced the Spirit. Each time you experience the swelling of your heart with the emotional burning in your chest that may rise in your throat; feel tears falling from truths heard from a moving sermon or a beautiful hymn; a thought that pops into your mind out of the blue, accompanied with a flood of emotion or perfect clarity; or are awakened with a thought that throws you into tears from its great meaning; you are experiencing the Spirit.

We need to learn how to recognize promptings, the small almost unnoticeable messages from the Spirit, and accurately decipher their meanings. To help you to begin recognizing if the Spirit is sending you a message or prompting, it is helpful to know that there are things that will always be contained in messages from God.

God primarily communicates with emotions and thoughts, which hold the total of its meaning, but they might contain one or two words of theme or topic said to your mind. These feelings may vary from loud and overwhelming to almost unnoticeably quiet and mild, and may hold a feeling of expectancy. They are usually at one or the other end of the extreme.

Generally, the Spirit always sends a total message. Once you recognize it, there will be no confusion about its meaning, whether it is a commendation or chastisement, an instruction, or information. You do need to focus on the thoughts and feelings that you experience, however. The thoughts and feelings, together, is the whole of the message. It is clear, and you know its whole meaning, no matter whether they are the quietest messages or those that are louder. Focus on your feelings and then your thoughts. You will miss part of the message if you only focus on one, thoughts or feelings, to the exclusion of the other. Once you notice both, thoughts and feelings, there will be no confusion of its meaning.

Foundationally, all messages from the Spirit make you feel closer to God and feel good about yourself—this is a confirmation telling you that it is a message from God and not one from any other source. This feeling is subdued, but you will notice it when you look to see its opposite—fear, shame, etc. All messages from God contain feelings of love—even chastisements. Even the largest chastisements that make you feel like you want to crawl under a rock contain great love. They do not make you feel afraid, only extremely humbled, clearly communicating to you that God commands you to change and letting you know what exactly it is, without question.

Recognizing the voice of the Spirit is far smaller (or larger) than you may anticipate. This smallness in volume is the hardest part of recognizing God's voice. I will try to accurately explain, from my perspective, the different ways that the Spirit speaks to me by using examples of my own chastisements. Hopefully seeing the different chastisements that I have received may help you to recognize his voice for yourself. Know that you will receive all types of messages, not just chastisements. I use my chastisements because they are the clearest examples of the types of messages given by the Spirit and so that you may compare them. Try to sense what you are feeling, as you read.

There are a few different ways that God speaks, in my experience. I differentiate the various messages to categorize them and to make it easier to explain. The quietest message from the Spirit is a *prompting*. I call it a *wondering*. I describe it as a *wondering* because it is so small that you wonder if God is speaking to you. While many people describe it as a *whisper* or a *whoosh*, I find that they are much smaller than that. I guess you could say that a prompting is a *whisper of a whisper*. It is so small that you may wonder if God is sending you a message. It is so small that you may think it is in your imagination. You may wonder if what you are hearing, thinking, and feeling *might* be a message from God, but that is the first clue. It is far smaller than what you think God's voice would be, but there is a wondering in the back of your mind that questions if God is speaking to you.

I find that a prompting usually contains no words but has an almost unnoticeable thought. The thought is not like a normal thought, but more like one being said in a voice smaller than a head of a pin that whispers from a great distance. To visualize it, I think about the Dr. Seuss book, *Horton Hears a Who*, how Horton barely hears the Who who is yelling from the Who world, which is on a speck of dust, which is sitting on top of a flower. You would not really hear it but it is a smaller thought that makes you wonder if someone is talking to you. If you notice it, you will barely notice, or you may not notice if you are not paying attention.

Instead, what you notice is a tiny feeling of anticipation, expectancy, urgency, or apprehension—it can feel like a tiny anxiety, without the negativity, that is uncomfortable and may not be completely noticed until it is gone. I usually notice that the feeling is gone after I have either received the message or have done what I was commanded to do, helping me to recognize that was indeed a message. It is much, much smaller than you would expect. I am surprised that I notice it at all. Of course, if I am thinking too much, it takes a while to figure out what the uncomfortable feeling is about. I feel the tiny feelings of apprehension across the whole of my chest and down to about my gut, where gut feelings originate, just below the breastbone and sternum. The feeling remains, helping me feel a bit uncomfortable until I do what I have been commanded to do. If I focus on the thought that comes with the uncomfortable feeling, I can sense a clue regarding the message part of the communication. This is the part of the message and instructions that you need to decipher, where the uncomfortable feeling is there to get you to notice. Once you focus on the feeling and search for its meaning, you will think of a topic. This is the message. You will wonder if God wants you to do something, or you will simply understand something. This is the message. Simply do what you wonder about. Once you have done it, the feelings of apprehension or anxiety will disappear, confirming that you received the message correctly.

I know that I have shared this particular chastisement before, but it taught me so much understanding. This chastisement was in a prompting. When I saw the bed bug on my bath towels and one on the floor, I was shocked and had to listen in order to recognize that I had received a chastisement. I was given it four times because I did not understand what I was doing wrong—or that I was doing something wrong at all. While it took me four times to figure it out, I immediately responded, asked questions, and asked for guidance and help. Finally, I told God that I must have done something wrong because he is incapable of making a mistake, so the mistake must be mine. I know I am fallible. After my prayer, tiny prompted hints were put into my mind about the timing of each chastisement and the number of times I had done the particular behavior, which gave me the clues to figure the answer. Once I said that I would stop doing the behavior, the chastisements stopped.

God was patient with me as I figured out what I was doing wrong because I immediately responded to God's command and tried to correct it, even though it took me four times to figure it out. God knew that I did not understand. My response to his chastisements, each time, made all the difference so that the consequences did not get worse, which may have if I had neglectfully ignored them.

While the quietest messages from the Spirit are promptings, I call the next kind a *message*. Messages may contain a one or two word theme or topic or may not contain any words at all. Messages are louder thoughts or insights that come into your mind at the same volume as your regular thoughts, where promptings are so quiet that you may think it is in your imagination; but you also receive emotions that either throw you into tears from its wealth of information, or they can be very mild. These messages can be considered to be *whooshes* or *whispers*. I find that I received these types of messages early on when learning to recognize the Spirit, when I received a chastisement, or when I have done something very difficult and God wanted to let me know that I did well.

I received another chastisement that was very powerful, and of which I would consider a *message*. It was far larger than a prompting although I actually heard nothing, but understood the thought clearly. I had been awakened in the middle of the night (about 3:30 am). The chastisement was strong enough to wake me and kept me from falling back asleep. I felt so much guilt that I wanted to crawl under a rock (yes, this is a real phenomenon). While the message was silent, the understanding of what I was doing wrong was completely clear in my mind, and the feelings were overwhelming. Even though the feelings were powerful and devastating, I also felt my Father's love. It felt as though I had disappointed him greatly, but that he loved me and commanded that I stop my behavior. I stopped the behavior immediately and did not repeat it. Just as I told him that I would stop, the chastisement and the feeling of wanting to crawl under a rock disappeared, although I still felt its sting, so I did not forget.

Sometimes the Spirit actually speaks, saying words to your mind. You hear the words clearly, as clearly as if someone is standing next to you and they speak to you, but you hear it in your mind and not your ears. I usually call this kind of message the *Spirit speaking to me*, because you hear words said in your mind. Like the *messages*, emotional information is given that may be quiet, or be a flood of emotional information. It can also hold all of the same types of things that messages do, but you hear information said to your mind.

I recall a time, many years ago, when I was lost and wandering in the wrong direction on my life path. I would not say that I was rebelling against God because I have never actively rebelled against God, or anyone else, for that matter. I was definitely lost and could not find the right way. I was even physically stopped from continuing what I was doing. Even though I did not recognize it as Spirit, at the time, I heard the voice clearly ask in my mind, "What do you want?" With no context and very little emotional information given (I did not recognize any, anyway), I only thought about the frustration and fatigue I was feeling from moving house. I wanted it to be done so I could rest. I did not consider that it was God asking the question. Answering, I said, "But, I want this." Immediately, he let go and allowed me to have my way, even loosening the physical barrier. A year later, I lost nearly everything I owned, walking away with only my car and very few of my belongings, although my belongings were the smallest part of my losses. Yet, I learned a very valuable lesson that day that I have not forgotten. My default answer to the question "What do you want?" is "Thy will be done!" I often wonder what would have happened if I would have answered the question differently.

The last type of messages received is just information, usually given while I sleep. This type I call a *download of information* because a download of wisdom or understanding was given. If it was given through the night, I notice the understanding when I awake, but I have received them during the day, too. This could be considered an *enlightenment*. I go to sleep not knowing the information and awake completely understanding it, as if all knowledge and wisdom about a specific topic was downloaded in my understanding. I may receive a short one or two word message whispered to my mind, in the morning, but mostly it contained no words. If one or two words are said to my mind, I hear them clearly, as clearly as someone saying my name, but I hear it in my mind, not in my ears. The information holds no words, only complete understanding—wisdom. The emotional information may be either small or may be overwhelming and vast.

All messages contain an element of emotion. The emotions felt are usually of two extremes, however. There are either the tiny feelings of urgency or expectancy that serves to only make me uncomfortable so that I notice, a simple feeling of peace and love, or the other extreme that is overwhelming and either feels like an earthquake of disappointment or all of the love and pride of God, holding the total complete meaning of what God wants me to know.

"For the word of God is quick, and powerful, and sharper than any two edged sword, piercing even to the dividing asunder of soul and spirit, and of the joints and marrow, and is a discerner of the thoughts and intents of the heart." (Hebrews 4:12 KJV)

You may find that God speaks with you mainly in a specific location or time. Most of my communications come at night, while I sleep (although promptings happen at any time). I know someone who receives answers to prayers in the bathroom. It seems that this is when she slows down long enough so that she can notice them. I have heard others tell of a whoosh of feeling and information, or a flash of enlightenment. Others hear words whispered in their minds. I met a woman who had the experience of hearing God call her by name, with associated feelings and information.

I have had many people ask how you know the message is from God or from another source (perhaps Satan or his angels). The devil can also communicate with you and may make it sound like it is coming from God. You can easily decipher between messages from God or from any other source.

1. Evil is much louder than Spirit. God communicates with us in promptings and whispers, and the whispers become quieter as you learn to tune into his voice more concisely. Evil's voice is louder, it can be frighteningly loud and shrill.

2. Evil cannot read your heart, and so the devil uses more words to communicate. God reads your mind and heart (God "is a discerner of the thoughts and intents of the heart"), and communicates with far fewer words, if any, using emotions to communicate, in your heart. On the other hand, the emotions evoked from evil would be feelings of guilt, fear, shame, etc. Satan can never send you feelings of peace, love, humility, or any other feelings that would make you feel better about you, or bring you closer to your Savior; and Spirit can never send negative or frightening emotions, or feelings that make you feel bad about you or Jesus. Plus, the feelings of peace, love, and humility felt from God are deeper and much larger than

anything we could produce in our imaginations, and may push you into tears with overwhelming love, humility, or righteous pride; or the feelings of expectancy and urgency would be so small that you barely notice or wonder if God is speaking to you. It is the extremes at each end of the spectrum.

3. Evil wants to confuse you; where God's communications are always clear, with complete understanding.

4. God always honors your agency, commanding you to do something, but allows you to choose, all ensuring that whatever he commands is good for all involved; where the devil demands things that are harmful, against the law, would cause problems for you or others, and do evil deeds, trying to take your agency. Evil would also make the fear bigger and stronger so that it can control and force you to do its will. God, on the other hand, commands. Demand tries to control, taking away agency; where command honors agency but lets you know that he means business.

5. Most importantly, God's communications always make you feel closer to Jesus without fear; where Satan makes you feel shameful to be close to him, trying to force you to stay far away from him, demanding that you stop praying, and tries to force you to believe that you are worthless and that Jesus does not love you any longer.

Focusing on your feelings and assessing whether you feel peace and love or fear and confusion helps you decipher the source from the message. The bottom line is that with each message, feel and listen. Use your spiritual barometer from the chapter, 'Belief is a Choice,' to tell if it is good or bad, or ask for a stupor.

A necessary thing to know about communications from God is that he does not argue (yes, I learned this the hard way, too). God sends you the message and that is it. In fact, there was only one time when he sent a subsequent message. The first time he commanded that I stop a behavior, telling me that he could remove the protection of bed bugs in my apartment if I did not stop, I said, mostly in my mind, that "I did not know he was protecting me." He sent a second message saying,

"You asked me to...." You may go back and forth, arguing and reasoning within yourself, but God's commands are firm and that is it—you will not receive further instructions.

I had decided to do something that I was not sure whether or not it would go against God's will. Praying about it and not receiving a *basic stupor*, which I requested, I decided to go ahead (this was before I had figured out about a *double-edged stupor*, and was one of the experiences that led me to think about how to receive God's will both ways—for and against). As I moved toward my plans, I had the opportunity to change my plans to do something that was longer and more challenging. As we started planning it, I had a wondering that clearly felt like he was telling me that my book (this book) would be taken away if I escalated it to the next level. The wondering was smaller than any other prompting that I had received before, so I thought it was my imagination. "But I want to!" I said, sitting for several minutes. "I did not actually hear him say it, like I did before," I reasoned. "But what if this feeling really was God?" I questioned the other side of the argument. "He is able to take the book away. Am I really willing to take that risk?" "He would not really take the book, would he?" Then I said the words again, "but I really want to do this!" Then, I realized what I had said. I said that I wanted my will over his—again. I felt a shock go right through me. I had to correct it fast! I took a deep breath to center my thoughts and humble myself. Bowed my head, I said, "Thy will be done." Even if it was my imagination, I did not want to go through the devastation that I knew would always follow if I chose my will over God's will. Immediately after I had said the words, the tiny feelings of urgency and chastisement disappeared, which I had not notice until it was gone, letting me know that it was a prompting of the Spirit—shocking me again from the realization of what I almost did. Because I knew how much I wanted to try the more challenging course and knowing how much God was against my doing it, I cancelled my plans, deleted the information, and even ended my acquaintances with the people with whom I had made my plans. Then I put a sticky note on my computer, on my bathroom mirror, and on the front door as a reminder of this chastisement. I did not want to forget.

As you learn to fine tune the hearing of the Spirit's voice, his voice gets quieter. The Spirit teaches you to tune into God's frequency even more precisely. This is how we learn to anticipate a message from God and fine tune into his frequency to hear clearer; even though the volume is very small¾even though we do not hear and there is no volume (there are any other words to express the experience of receiving God's messages). This is what Abraham would have learned so that he immediately responded to God's messages and obeyed any requested tasks, no matter what was asked of him.

Your message from God may hold a request for you to do something. Simply do it. These requests feel like promptings to urge you to comply. The feeling subsides once the task is done, telling you that it was a prompting. You do not receive much, if any, additional information until you have done the requested task, and then you might not receive additional information at all. The most common types of tasks requested would be to use faith before you receive knowledge or a blessing— usually in a test of your faith. These are very seemingly insignificant tasks, but you will gain the full understanding after you complete it. If you are concerned about the source of the requested task, pray about it. Know that it will never be anything that is against the law, is evil, or inequitable. They are not scary; instead you feel the small feelings of peace, through the urgency. Feel for the feelings of peace and simply do it. If you are still concerned about the source of your request, ask for a stupor to remove it if it is against God's will for you to do it, asking to remove the anxiety about doing it. This is an *oblivion stupor*, and will happen immediately, so that you know what you should do.

Recognizing the Spirit's voice will be the most challenging part of developing life-changing faith. It is not difficult. In fact, we need to recognize its simplicity and feel for the possibilities. In our imperfect life, we focus on the impossible, ignoring the possible. Jesus is all about what is possible, as you will learn soon. If we focus on the smallest thought that he may be speaking to you, sending you a message, prompting you to do something, etc., keeping that possibility channel in your mind and heart, you would be doing what Abraham did, always listening and anticipating God's voice. Messages from our Father in heaven and Savior may be tossed aside as unimportant imaginations of thought, they are so small, but you would have thrown away the most important and precious treasures that you can receive, simply by not understanding that this is how deity speaks.

Recognizing the Spirit's voice and disciplining yourself to comply with his instructions is the single most empowering thing you can do to develop life-changing faith. Please know that our Father in heaven and Savior are very patient as we learn to recognize the Spirit's voice. I have made so many mistakes and missed so many messages. They give us other opportunities to learn and do it better next time.

We receive so many blessings from this one aspect of life-changing faith that is very valuable. Putting the small amount of effort to learn to recognize the Spirit's voice is more than worth it. Remember, the Spirit cannot bless you unless your sins are forgiven, so promptings and messages from the Spirit are little reminders that all of your sins have been forgiven, you are on the right road, and are ripe to receive the blessings that you request from God.

9

WHAT IS FAITH?

**"That your faith should not stand in the wisdom
of men, but in the power of God."
(1 Corinthians 2:5 KJV)**

As we address the last misconceptions standing in the way of developing life-changing faith, find out what faith actually is, and begin using our newly-developed tools to expand and grow our faith, and gain the blessings we desire, it is essential to understand the wisdom and power of simplicity, or at least accept it. Simplicity is the key to the gospel of Jesus Christ. Those who understood it, the humble, are those who followed Jesus throughout his ministry. In the chapter, 'Belief is a Choice,' we learned that any concept that is simple, enlightening, and brings us closer to our Father in heaven and our Savior, without fear, is good and is of God; and any concept that takes you away from them and causes you to fear or makes you feel bad about yourself, is evil. We identified that this is our spiritual barometer that clearly shows us if it, whatever it is, is truth or lie, good or evil; for anything that is evil will not bring us closer to our Savior, where anything that is good will not take us from him. With that in mind, we begin to put things together to develop life-changing faith.

What is faith? Faith is a belief, a confidence that the belief is true to the point of action, as if you had already received proof (Hebrews 11:1 KJV). This is the basic definition of faith. Of course, we know that the being in which we believe, yet has not provided evidence as proof of his existence, in our lifetime, anyway, is our Savior, Jesus Christ. It is the Christ in whom we believe and in whom we put our trust, our confidence, and our faith. We place our belief, hope, and trust in him because he has provided a perfect example of how to live our lives in such a way that we may return to our Father in heaven, and through his infinite atonement and sacrifice, we may receive redemption from our sins.

Faith in the Lord, Jesus Christ places us in a position of confidence. We may confidently lay claim to the blessings that await those who put their faith in Jesus; the wonderful blessings about which we read in the pages of the Bible. Through faith in Jesus Christ we are able to do all things. This power is given as a result of developing life-changing faith and is the life-changing part of our faith. This means that all blessings, both spiritual and temporal, may be wrought by faith. This is not universally accepted nor understood, based on the number of times the Bible lists all that faith can accomplish, commands us to ask that we may receive, and our inability to successfully get our faith to *work*. Whether we understand how to use our faith or not, faith is a power that through Jesus' name we are able to make things happen for ourselves and our loved ones. Faith is an active power, not a passive one.

Faith is something that man uses to please God. This is also not universally accepted nor understood. Because we may please God and be seen as worthy in his sight, we are justified, purified, and will ultimately be sanctified and perfected through our faith in the Savior, just as Abraham, Rahab, and many others were; and just as Jesus has shown us that he was perfected through faith in himself, as the Christ, for even he had faith in himself.

> "What doth it profit, my brethren, though a man say he hath faith, and have not works? can faith save him? If a brother or sister be naked, and destitute of daily food, And one of you say unto them, Depart in peace, be ye warmed and filled; notwithstanding ye give them not those things which are needful to the body; what doth it profit? *Even so faith, if it hath not works, is dead, being alone.* Yea, a man may say, Thou hast faith, and I have works: shew me thy faith without thy works, and

I will shew thee my faith *by my works.* Thou believest that there is one God; thou doest well: the devils also believe, and tremble. But wilt thou know, O vain man, that faith without works is dead? Was not Abraham our father justified by works, when he had offered Isaac his son on the altar? Seest thou how *faith wrought with his works, AND by works was faith made perfect?* And the scripture was fulfilled which saith, Abraham believed God, and it was imputed unto him for righteousness: and he was called the Friend of God. Ye see then how that by works a man is justified, and not by faith only. Likewise, also was not Rahab the harlot justified by works, when she had received the messengers, and had sent them out another way? For as the body without the spirit is dead, so faith without works is dead also." (James 2:14–26 KJV, italics and capitalization added)

I do not know why these verses are so controversial. These verses clearly illustrate that faith propels us to action and that we are justified, in God's judgment, by the righteous acts caused by faith. These verses may cause confusion as we try to address the complexities of language (and James' passion), yet they hold very simple truths.

While we are talking about faith, and sin and forgiveness seems to be off topic, our faith is tied to our judgment. Truth tells us that we are saved by the grace of God, through the atonement of Jesus Christ. There is nothing that we are able to do, on our own, to be redeemed (saved). This is a gift freely given and without price to all people. Through his grace, we have the ability to repent and be forgiven, and eventually be saved from our sinful natures. Redemption is the liberation of our sins— the *ability* to be forgiven. We need repentance to actually be forgiven from our sins, which is an act, a work. That being said, because we are capable of sinning again, because we are human, we are not truly clean. We can be forgiven but we are only purified by becoming like Jesus, which is another work—yes, we may do some of this work while in this life.

Struggling against our sinful nature and learning to change those parts of us that are imperfect, doing more than emulating Jesus, but changing ourselves to be more like him, we are purified. In only this way can we clean parts of us *by our works,* which still does not negate the necessity of the atonement because we will never be truly clean until the atonement cleans our sinful natures, after this life. Obeying promptings of the Spirit, bearing a prompted witness, helping someone in need, and other things done in Jesus' name to do good, changes parts of us to become more like Jesus. In this way we are doing things *by our works.* While we can be justified (absolved, excused) when we repent and do good works, we must continue struggling against our sinful natures until we are judged. After we have answered for the words and deeds of our lives and are judged, then we may be purified (cleansed of the ability to sin) and sanctified (consecrated, perfected, made holy). We can be justified, purified and sanctified because the combination of our works (all that we do in Jesus' name) and our faith (the belief and trust in Jesus) makes our faith perfect, as we discipline ourselves to do those things that our faith propels us to do.

> "Was not Abraham our father justified by works, when he had offered Isaac his son upon the altar? Seest thou how faith wrought with his works, and by works was faith made perfect?" (James 2:21–22 KJV)

While our works alone cannot save us, and our faith is dead without our works, our works animate and enliven our faith. Our works are the nutrition that our faith needs. It must start with our agency, for faith dies, sitting in our selfish natures. Doing good in Jesus' name makes us more like him, which cleans us from our selfish natures, which strengthens and grows our faith as a blessing from God. Adding them together, our faith, our works, and the atonement (for we cannot do it for ourselves), perfects our faith in Jesus. Our faith in Jesus Christ and becoming like him, and the atonement of Jesus' sacrifice, together, shall justify, purify, and will ultimately sanctify us, by perfecting our faith. Again, it is all about Jesus.

Faith is a power that propels us to action. To change hope into faith requires action. Hope is not what we think it is. We think that hope is a longing wish. This is not hope. Actually, hope is an anticipation that is associated with trust—the expectancy that we feel before we create the plan of action done in faith. Acting on that trust of hope creates faith. Faith is an action, and using faith requires action, or it stays as a wish.

God propels us, through promptings, to do things for his purposes, and faith propels us to do them. We have heard of stories of people driving home from work and being prompted to stop and purchase a gallon of milk. Then, as they neared their homes, they were prompted to turn down a different street, stop in front of a specific house and bring the milk to that home to find a family whose baby had not eaten all day, was very hungry and crying, and a mother who was also crying because she did not have the means to purchase any milk. These types of actions justify these people in the sight of God. We know this because the Spirit prompted and they obeyed, just as Abraham did as he took Isaac to sacrifice him.

Our righteous works seal and perfect our faith. Many people are able to talk big, but they fall short even thinking about doing something. Our actions tell us much more than our words, so to do that which we believe and not only passively believe, sets the concrete to our faith; for we only truly believe when we act according to that which we believe. To develop life-changing faith, our faith must propel us to act. But know that this is a simple and easy thing to do. The reward of doing so strengthens and grows your faith very quickly. We must recognize the promptings of the Spirit and act on them.

Even a basic faith is enough to gain favor with the Father.

> "If ye have faith as a grain of mustard seed, ye shall say unto this mountain, Remove hence to yonder place; and it shall remove; and nothing shall be impossible to you." (Matthew 17:20 KJV)

> "But without faith it is impossible to please him: for he that cometh to God must believe that he is, and [that] he is a rewarder of them that diligently seek him." (Hebrews 11:6 KJV)

Comparing these two verses lets us know that a basic faith is all that is required "and nothing shall be impossible to you." That means that miracles can be a daily occurrence, once you understand the truth about faith.

Miracles are a subject about which many Christians love hearing, but many do not believe, in this age. Yet blessings that we deem as miraculous may be simple blessings from a loving and powerful God. Of course, there are large miracles, such as Joshua praying that the sun would stop in the sky for a day. This is not the type of miracles that we discuss here. But if we received a clear and unmistakable prompting from the Spirit, God is able to bring these types of miracles to us, too, for his purposes. Usually, large miracles are requested by a prophet, since it is done for or on behalf of a whole people. Here, we talk about miracles that can be part of your daily life; the miracles of healing, help, and wisdom that we may want and need in our lives—the personal miracles, instead of the miracles of a whole people.

Many believe that there are no miracles in this day. I tell you that miracles can be part of your daily life. Those who have developed life-changing faith experience miracles as a regular part of their everyday lives.

> "He that believeth and is baptized shall be saved; but he that believeth not shall be damned. And these signs shall follow them that believe; In my name shall they cast out devils; they shall speak with new tongues; they shall take up serpents; and if they drink any deadly thing, it shall not hurt them; they shall lay hands on the sick, and they shall recover." (Mark 16:16–18 KJV)

These verses do not tell what only the apostles of old were able to do, but these types of miracles, and many others, help us to identify those who have developed life-changing faith, because they are part of their lives.

To say that God is no longer a God of miracles is to more accurately say that none of us have developed faith in Jesus, or that they have been so blinded by their misconceptions that they no longer know how to develop or use it. If miracles have ceased then God is a liar, for the Bible tells us that God is the same yesterday, today, and forever (Malachi 3:6 KJV, Hebrews 13:8 KJV, Revelation 1:8 KJV). If miracles have ceased than we all have distanced ourselves from Jesus, which is a serious sin. If miracles have ceased then it is because faith has ceased also, having hardened our hearts against Jesus. If faith has ceased then man has lost its hope in the Savior's atonement, his ability to save, and is in a state of despair. Despair is a sin because hope in the Savior is gone.

I testify to you that miracles have not ceased! Miracles are an essential and natural part of the development of life-changing faith. While we see miracles as huge and magical occurrences, miracles are simple blessings from a powerful God. It is as easy for God to stop the rotation of the earth for a day and part the Red Sea so that the Israelites may pass on dry land as it is for him to prompt a member of a family, who has proven as an enemy, to pay for unexpected automobile repairs (I have had this miracle). If we do not experience miracles in our lives, we are doing or believing something very wrong. Miracles can be part of each one of our lives, as we grow and use life-changing faith.

Mark stated that miracles follow those who have great faith. The only requirement to experience miracles, in your lives, is that you need to believe: "And these signs shall follow them that believe….". So, if you do not experience miracles and have corrected the misconceptions regarding faith that we have discussed thus far, you must have the last remaining misconception that will immediately open your heart and understanding to the faith that will change your life. These blessings will be miraculous in your life and will serve to grow and strengthen your faith.

While miracles cannot create faith, for faith is created by our agency (a will to believe and trust), miracles have a confirming and empowering effect on it. They also cause a craving for more of the Spirit and the need to be even closer to Jesus, all the while being humbled and growing confident by and with him at the same time. Since miracles further increase faith and testimony, they are necessary to bring more people to Christ. Whatsoever things are beneficial to the building of the Kingdom of God, and helps to increase faith and trust in the Savior, are expedient. Since blessings and miracles bring us closer to Jesus, without fear, we see that they are good and true.

We see the word *expedient* now and again in the Bible. This word is an interesting word that has great meaning. We think that *expedient* means *necessary*, but it also means *practical, useful, beneficial,* and *appropriate*. It is expedient for us to glorify Jesus as he glorifies the Father, for this is how more of his children are brought to Christ. Great faith is expedient, as are the miracles and other gifts from God because they promote, strengthen, and increase faith.

Before we address the last remaining misconception of faith, there is another almost hidden, aspect of faith that cannot be overlooked. We find it in the writings of St. Luke.

> "And it came to pass, as he went to Jerusalem, that he passed through the midst of Samaria and Galilee. And as he entered into a certain village, there met him ten men that were lepers, which stood afar off: and they lifted up their voices and said, Jesus, Master, have mercy on us. And when he saw them, he said unto them, Go shew yourselves unto the priests. And it came to pass, that, as they went, they were cleansed. And one of them, when he saw that he was healed, turned back, and with a loud voice glorified God. And fell down on his face at his feet, giving him thanks; and he was a Samaritan. And Jesus answered said, Were there not ten cleansed? But where are the nine? There are not found that returned to give glory to God, save this stranger. And he said unto him, Arise, go thy way: thy faith hath made thee whole." (Luke 17:11–19 KJV)

This story shows us another element of faith: Gratitude. We must hold a spirit of gratitude in the asking and the receiving of our Father's blessings. Gratitude is part of worship and faith. In Old Testament times, there were Thank Offerings offered on altars in the temple. Gratitude is a law that required a blood sacrifice, in ancient times, and is a law that is required of us today. While the remission of sins was a required sacrifice, the Thank Offering was a voluntary offering to show gratitude (Leviticus 7:11-15 KJV). The Thanksgiving offering was part of the Peace offering, which required a blood sacrifice. Today, gratitude is still a voluntary offering, illustrating a thankful and gracious heart, returning back to the giver of blessings in humble and heart-felt thanksgiving.

Blessings from God should never be taken for granted. We must always return back in thanks and praise for the blessings received. This law is not difficult to follow. When blessings and miracles are received, it is nearly impossible not to feel great humility and deep gratitude associated with receiving them. It is possible, however, to go on without giving it much thought, content in the receipt of the blessings, complacently forgetting to formally thank the Father. It is necessary, even if it is days, weeks, months, or years later, to remember and return to God in a prayer of gratitude for the blessing received, thanking him for each one specifically if we are able.

Let us put everything together to develop life-changing faith.

10

ARE YOU ABLE TO DO
THIS THING?

**"I know whom I have believed, and am persuaded that he is
able to keep that which I have committed unto him against
that day. Hold fast the form of sound words, which thou hast
heard of me, in faith and love which is in Christ Jesus."
(2 Timothy 1:12-13)**

There are ways that faith must be used that many do not understand today. Whether the traditions and knowledge have not been passed down from generation to generation as they were in ancient times, or most do not read or understand their Bible as they should, it is unclear how this knowledge was lost. You will know the truth and you will read your Bible with new eyes. The truth certainly sets you free. There is a foundational seed to your faith that when utilized, puts you in line with Bible teachings and the requirements of faith sufficient to bring about miracles in your life—instantly. Note: in this chapter, I will be using the term *God* generally, but it could pertain both to our Father in heaven and Jesus.

We have been instructed that we must have a firm, unwavering, and unshakable faith. How is that possible? We have been told in Sunday school and from the pulpit (and on social media sites) that faith is the belief that God will bless us. Yet, we learned in the chapter, 'God's Will and Our Faith,' that God's will is his alone, and that we are to submit our will to him because we cannot, and nor should we, manipulate God.

Faith is far simpler and easier to accomplish than this. While the belief that God will bless us is part of an advanced faith that will come as you use life-changing faith, it may not be possible for many of us to believe that God will bless us because of past experiences of not receiving requested blessings, false beliefs, concerns about worthiness, or dozens of other reasons. Since there are some of God's children who may not be able to achieve this belief, the belief to develop faith must be far simpler than this so that *all* may achieve the requirements. They need the foundational seed or key of faith.

Looking at the life of our Savior, he did all things by using the principle of faith. He showed faith when he spoke with people. He used faith when he healed them. He used faith when he materialized enough bread and fishes to feed thousands and had extra, from a few. He used faith when he walked on water and told Peter that if he believed, he could do it, too. He used faith when he went to the Father and communicated for his will to raise the dead. All things were done with a firm confidence. He was the exemplar of faith.

When we read about the life of the Savior, particularly the records of Jesus' earthly ministry, we are given hints to the foundational seed of faith near each healing he performed. This foundational seed of faith tells us how we can activate our faith sufficient to ask for and receive blessings from God (yes, we need to activate our faith). If we pay close attention, for the key is hidden in plain sight, we are able to gain clues about what this foundational seed of faith is, and how to develop and activate powerful life-changing faith immediately. Remember that if you have a seed, and do not plant it and nurture it, it will remain useless, no matter how powerful it's potential.

In each record, near almost every healing, Jesus asked one question of each of those whom he healed. Look. Are you able to pick out the question? Is there ever anything recorded in the Bible where Jesus said (I hear this in a tough-guy Brooklyn accent), "Come on, tell me how much you want me to heal you," or "prove to me that you are deserving of my healing touch, and then I'll think about it." No. But Jesus did ask one thing of each of those with whom he healed. What did Jesus ask?

Explaining the foundational seed of faith, I asked several people what Jesus asked to everyone he healed. Most said that he asked if their faith was sufficient for a healing. Is this what he asked? No, not at all. This is the meaning that we put to his words. Since the Savior did nothing arbitrarily, we need to look at his actual words, rather than to our own interpretation. His actual words hold the foundational seed of faith.

Jesus asked every person he healed if they believed that he was able to do the thing which they asked. Take a look. The blind men, those with leprosy, even the woman who touched the hem of his garment had to acknowledge that they believed that Jesus was able to heal them—the woman who had hemorrhaged for twelve years clearly admitted in her mind that she believed he was able. Each person who Jesus healed was required to acknowledge, in some way, that they believed that he was able to heal them.

While some may think that there is no difference between these people acknowledging that they believed Jesus was able and admitting that their faith was sufficient for the healing, there is a huge difference. Jesus did not ask if their faith was sufficient for the healing because, like our Father in heaven, he was able to read their hearts and see for himself if they possessed such faith—the Bible records some of them (Mark 2:5 KJV, Luke 5:20 KJV); plus Jesus saw the blasphemy in the hearts of the Pharisees. Because Jesus did nothing arbitrarily, his exact words, what he actually asked of each person and why, holds great meaning and purpose.

What is the purpose for his asking all those who Jesus healed if they believed he was able to do that which they asked? Looking at the recorded life of the Savior, his entire life reflected this one thing, that he is able. As Jesus moved about and taught truths to the people, he moved with the firm, unwavering, unshakable belief that he is able. He healed the sick and the lame, healing all diseases in all people who came to him, through the power of faith in himself, as the Son of God, God on Earth, knowing that he is able to do all things. He cast demons and devils from people through the power of faith in himself, knowing that he was able to do so. He walked on water, turned water into wine, and raised those who had died. Of course he knew. Why would he not know that he was able? He created the earth, the universe, and all that were in them before his life. He fed the thousands (five thousand men plus women and children) with a measly five loaves of bread and two fishes through his faith that he was able. He replaced the ear of a palace guard, through belief that he was able, as they went to the garden to take him to Pilate. Praying at Gethsemane, he took on himself all the sins and sufferings of the world, surviving the literal breaking of his heart, at the weight, through his firm, unwavering, and unshakable belief that he was able. He survived the torture, mocking, and the depravity of man and hell, with a firm, unwavering, and unshakable belief that he was able to continue until the atonement was complete. He hung on the cross and waited until long after the others, hanging beside him, were dead (long after any man had ever lived on the cross), as a testament that no man took his life, but that he gave it freely. Then, of his own will and control, through a firm, unwavering, and unshakable belief in his ability to do so, he commanded his spirit from his body, giving his life as a sacrifice and blood testimony that he is the Messiah, finishing his earthly mission, and fulfilling all prophecies from all prophets from the beginning of time. Then Jesus arose from the tomb on the third day, opening the gates of death to begin the resurrection of souls, being the first, with a firm, unwavering and unshakable belief that he is Jesus Christ and he is able to do even that. Jesus held a firm, unwavering, unshakable belief that he was able. Those things for with which he consulted the Father, he submitted to the Father's will and still held that firm, unwavering, and unshakable belief that he was able, thereby setting the prime and perfect example for us to follow.

Our loving and merciful God wants for all of us to return to him. Faith is the requirement to return to God and so he ensured that they be simple enough so that all would have the ability to successfully achieve it—the child as well as the elder (all ages), the kindergartener as well as the PhD (uneducated as well as the educated), the sinner and the saint (no matter where they are on life's path), Adam and the last baby to be born (all throughout all time), the poor as well as the wealthy (all can afford), the genius as well as the challenged (all abilities)—all have the ability to be saved by faith in Jesus Christ by believing that he is able.

Now, I give you a strong warning: Do not do as some of the Israelites did who refused to look to the brass serpent and live (Numbers 21 KJV). This key is simple—too simple—yet it possesses the power sufficient to develop life-changing faith *because* of its simplicity, and *because* all are able to use it successfully—it is full of equity. It is how you use this key that brings the magic to your faith, and truly makes your faith life-changing.

Before we get into how to use this understanding to bless you and your family's lives, what do you personally believe about Jesus' ability to do all things? Please answer each of these questions, deeply thinking about what you truly believe, as you read them. This is important. Do not simple read them, but answer them, even in your thoughts. Do you believe that Jesus possesses power over all of the earth, all that is in it, and the entire universe? Do you believe that he created your body, and therefore, is able to repair it? Do you believe that he possesses all knowledge and wisdom? Do you believe that he is able to forgive all of your sins? Do you believe that he is able to bestow blessings? Do you believe that he is able to send you miracles? Do you believe that he is able to heal diseases and suffering? When answering these questions, do not think about your thoughts or beliefs about his *willingness*; answer them only with your belief about his *ability*. If you do not believe in God, do not believe that he is real, or doubt that he is there, instead of answering, "Do you believe that God is able...," answer these questions with, "If there is a God, would he be able to...." For those who doubt or those who have not had enough experience to know God, understanding that God wants all of us to return to him, changing the question is necessary and expedient.

Answer these questions before moving on—this is important.

In the chapter, 'God's Will and Our Faith,' we learned that God's will is his alone. We understand that we have to meet the requirements of our faith while allowing God's will to remain his; meaning that we need to meet the requirements of our faith by ourselves—by our agency—and do so equitably, for *all* people. Using the foundational seed of faith puts *all* people in a position to be able to develop life-changing faith and giving all people the accessibility of salvation through Christ. This distinction is equitable and perfect, creating no bias against or preference toward any person(s). This distinction, if tested as instructed in the Bible, is the first huge step to developing life-changing faith, and creates the faith sufficient to bring miracles to your life, immediately.

The Bible tells us that our faith must be firm, unwavering, and unshakable, but how can we achieve this requirement? First, we need to assess how firmly we believe that Jesus is able. Think about how firmly you believe that God is able to do all things. Think about a blessing that you would like God to bless you with now. It could be to gain wisdom about a specific topic; or to be healed, like Jesus did during his life. It could be any righteous desire. Thinking about that blessing, do you believe that God is able to do that thing? How firmly do you believe?

Knowing that God is able to create our bodies gives us the firm faith that he is able to repair it. Knowing that God created this and other universes, and all things therein, gives us the firm faith that he is able to move things about and instruct us by which power they move. Knowing that God is able gives us the firm faith that he is able to do all things, which sets us up for success by placing our faith on a very firm foundation. Do you remember the parable about the house set on the sand or rock? This sets your faith on *diamonds*¾the firmest foundation on earth (Matthew 7:24–27 KJV). Even someone who questions the validity of God is able to have enough faith because they understand that if there is a God, he would be able to do all things. Even the unbeliever has the possibility to have the foundational requirements of faith sufficient to ask for and receive blessings from God, thus giving yet another of God's lost lambs an opportunity to gain belief and faith in Jesus.

As we begin to use our faith, we do not need to hold out an impossible firm, unwavering, and unshakable hope that God will do what we ask to have life-changing faith. Holding out hope does not contain the power that holding a firm faith is required for miracles to happen in our lives. We can, however, hold out hope that God will bless us, while firmly knowing that he is able.

In 2005, the experience occurred that started my journey to understanding faith. I had been suffering with a great deal of anxiety. My thoughts raced like a thirty-lane race track with no speed limit, no set direction, no lane markers, and bumper-to-bumper traffic, all going more than 200 miles per hour, returning to be replayed over and over and over again (my life felt like an old silent black-and-white cops and robbers movie). Day and night, night and day, I could not slow my mind, even to sleep. Desperate, I made an appointment at the university hospital's psychiatric department to ask for some help.

The doctor with whom I had the appointment talked to me for about two minutes and then told me that while I only exhibited one symptom, explaining that I was supposed to exhibit at least five of the seven symptoms to be diagnosed, he neglectfully prescribe bipolar medication, not even considering anxiety or post-traumatic stress disorder (PTSD) as an option, which I would later learn that it was. After trying three different pharmaceutical drugs, all of which had horrific side effects, one even slowing my speech to the point that it sounded like I had incurred a brain injury, I decided that the side effects were not worth the slower pace of my thoughts (which were far slower than I needed) and began weaning off of them. About three weeks after I had been off of the medication entirely, I began to experience my thoughts speed up again.

On my way to work, a thirteen-mile commute, after a sleepless night due to additional anxiety at my thoughts speeding up again, I sat behind the wheel of my car and began to pour my heart out to Jesus, as if he was in the passenger seat next to me. I told him that I was beginning to experience the racing thoughts again and that it was more than I could bear. I explained that I had not been able to sleep because of the volume and speed at which my thoughts raced, and that I had done all that I could do by trying meditation techniques, which I could not get to work; and seeing a doctor and trying three pharmaceutical drugs, all of which had horrible and debilitating side effects that prevented me from doing my job. I explained that I needed my job to support me and my children, and that I needed to be able to sleep to keep it (also explaining that I had been so cross with my children because of it all). With tears rolling down my cheeks, I tried to plead my case in the most powerful words that I could use, trying not to beg but to use logic in my words, as I explained.

I told him that I knew that he made my body so, of course, I knew he was able to repair it but that I did not know if he would. I told him that I wished that I was living during the time when he was on the earth so that I could do as the woman did who had hemorrhaged for twelve years. I told him that I, too, would find a doorway, wait for him to pass by, and reach out to touch the hem of his garment. I desired it so completely that I even visualized doing just that.

Just as I reached toward Jesus' sandaled feet to allow the hem of his garment to brush the top of my hand, in my imagination, I realized that I was no longer in control of my car but someone or some energy had taken control and was driving me to work, for me. I felt completely safe and at peace. There was no fear whatsoever, and I felt like I was in some kind of a trance; yet, all the same, I was fully aware of all that was happening around and in me.

There was a sensation in the upper left rear quarter of my head, under my skull—it felt as if someone was moving stuff around, up there. I continued seated in the driver's seat, my hands on the steering wheel and my eyes looking forward; the car still driving, uninterruptedly, safely, and legally toward my place of work, but I was not the one driving my car—or, perhaps, I was put on autopilot, kind of like the days when I have a lot on my mind and I do not remember driving, except that day I was aware. It drove all the way to work and even parked in the same parking space in which I usually parked, the gear put in Park and the ignition turned off. I saw colleagues walking from their cars to the elevator, as I sat.

I sat there for a few minutes after I came back into reality, feeling the residual sensation in my head, which stayed with me for several days. My mind was completely calm and I was at peace. My head felt as if I had surgery, although there was no pain—only the energy of what had happened there. I questioned the possibility of what I had just experienced. Is it possible that Jesus allowed me to touch the hem of his garment while I was driving my car? I could not deny what had happened, although I also had difficulty believing that it was possible—for me.

I slowly walked into work and sat at my desk, bewildered and humbled at the thought (only one) of what I had just experienced. I called my mother on the telephone, still in shock, and began recounting the happenings of that morning. She interrupted me and asked if he allowed me to touch the hem of his garment. I answered, "Yes." I cried at relating this most precious story to the only person I thought that would spiritually get it.

Pondering this occurrence later, trying to figure out what had happened and what I had done to spur the miracle, I turned to my Bible, to the life of the Savior, and began to read, hoping to find an answer. I began to read the story about the woman who had hemorrhaged for twelve years, being the story to which I felt so connected. Then I saw it, right in the verses just before this important story. I turned to other healings and it was there too. Right there on the pages was the question that Jesus asked, "Do you believe I am able to do this thing?" I realized that as soon as I spoke those words, "I know you are able, but I do not know if you will," I experienced the healing—and total protection while driving. I left God's will to his infinite wisdom and acknowledged what I knew to be true, that he was able to heal me, thereby activating my faith.

Jesus did not ask if they believed he was able to do what they asked of him because he did not know if they had any faith. He asked them to acknowledge their belief that he is able to activate their faith. Acknowledging their belief is an act of will (agency) and so they had to activate their faith before Jesus was able to heal them. Obviously, the woman who had hemorrhaged for twelve years had activated her faith by devising a plan, crouching in the doorway, and having the courage to put her hand out toward Jesus' feet, creating the action to turn her hope into faith. But she acknowledged in her mind that if she could even brush her hand against the hem of Jesus' robes, she would be healed.

Whether you know it or not, you have just activated your faith sufficient to bring miracles regarding the blessing you desire and thought about when asking yourself the question that Jesus asked of all those he healed. Answering the questions, acknowledging your belief, even in your mind, activated your faith. You may help others to also activate their faith by asking them the question, "Do you believe that God is able to... (adding what they desire or need)?" Acknowledging your belief that God is able, to what level you honestly believe, is the missing yet essential key to developing life-changing faith. We need to activate our faith. This is key.

The Bible instructs us that we must hold a firm, unwavering, unshakable faith and then anything that is asked will be done (Matthew 21:22 KJV, Mark 5:36 KJV, Hebrews 11:6, 17-40 KJV, Mark 11:23-24 KJV, James 1:5-6 KJV, Luke 1:37 KJV). Acknowledging that God is able answers the requirements for faith. We are able to hold a perfect faith in Christ, believing, nothing doubting that he is able (Hebrews 10:23 KJV, James 1:6 KJV). This answers all the misconceptions concerning faith, including the misconception of worthiness. Fears about your worthiness is usually wrapped up in not knowing if God is willing to answer your plea, but is answered in what you already know to be true—that he is able. This simply places you in a position of faith rather than any worry you may have. Ask, believing that God is able to grant that which you ask, is sufficient faith to bring about miracles and is congruent with Jesus' perfect example, recorded in the Bible.

Let us look at the Bible. Notice how many times these verses separate the will of the Lord from his abilities:

> "Wherefore *he is able* also to save them to the uttermost that come unto God by him, seeing he ever liveth to make intercession for them." (Hebrews 7:25 KJV, italics added)

> "For that ye ought to say, *If the Lord will, we shall* live." (James 4:15 KJV, italics added)

> "*If so be the Lord will* be with me, then *I shall be able* to drive them out, as the Lord said." (Joshua 14:12 KJV, italics added)

> "And the angel of the Lord appeared unto the woman, and said unto her, Behold now, *thou art baren*, and bearest not: *but thou shalt conceive*, and bear a son." (Judges 13:3 KJV, italics added)

> "If it be so, our God whom we serve *is able* to deliver us from the burning fiery furnace, and he will deliver us out of thine hand, O king.... Blessed be the God of Shadrach, Meshach, and Abed-nego, who hath sent his

angel, and delivered his servants that trusted in him, and have changed the king's word, and yielded their bodies, that they might not serve nor worship any God, except their own God...because there was no other God *that can deliver* after this sort. Then the king promoted Shadrach, Meshach, and Abed-nego, in the province of Babylon." (Daniel 3:17, 28–30 KJV, italics added)

"Daniel, O Daniel, servant of the living God, is thy God, whom thou servest continually, *able to deliver thee* from the lions? My God hath sent his angel, and hath shut the lions' mouths.... So Daniel was taken up out of the den, and no manner of hurt was found upon him, because he believed in his God." (Daniel 6: 20, 23 KJV, italics added)

"Think out to say within yourselves, We have Abraham to our father; for I say unto you, that *God is able* of these stones to raise up children unto Abraham." (Matthew 3:9 KJV, italics added)

"And the Lord said unto Abraham, Wherefore did Sarah laugh, saying, Shall I of a surety bear a child, which am old? Is any thing too hard for the Lord? At the time appointed I will return unto the, according to the time of life, and Sarah shall have a son." (Genesis 18:13-15 KJV)

"And, behold, there came a leper and worshipped him, saying, Lord, *if thou wilt, thou canst* make me clean. And Jesus put forth his hand, and touched him, saying, *I will; be thou clean.* And immediately his leprosy was cleansed." (Matthew 8:2–3 KJV, italics added)

"And, behold, a woman, which was diseased with a hemorrhage twelve years, came behind him, and touched the hem of his garment: for she knew within herself, If I may but touch his garment, *I shall be whole....* Thy faith hath made thee whole. And the woman was made whole from that hour." (Matthew 9:20–22 KJV, italics added.)

"And when Jesus departed thence, two blind men followed him, crying, and saying, Thou Son of David, have mercy on us. And when he was come into the house, the blind men came to him: and Jesus saith unto them, *Believe ye that I am able to do this?* They said unto him, Yea, Lord. Then, touched he their eyes saying, *According to your faith be it unto you.* And their eyes were opened." (Matthew 9:27–30 KJV, italics added)

"And when he had called unto him his twelve disciples, *he gave them power* against unclean spirits, to cast them out, and to heal all manner of sickness and all manner of disease." (Matthew 10:1 KJV, italics added)

"But the ship was now in the midst of the sea, tossed with waves: for the wind was contrary. And in the fourth watch of the night *Jesus went* unto them, walking on the sea." (Matthew 14:24–26 KJV, italics added)

"Then Jesus called his disciples unto him, and said, I have compassion on the multitude, because they continue with me now three days, and have nothing to eat: and *I will not* send them away fasting, lest they faint in the way.... *And he took* the seven loaves and the fishes, *and gave thanks, and brake them*, and gave to his disciples, and the disciples to the multitude. And they did all eat, and were filled: and they took up of the broken meat that was left seven baskets full. And they that did eat were four thousand men, beside women and children." (Matthew 15:32, 36–38 KJV, italics added)

"Go thou to the sea, and cast an hook, and take up the fish that first cometh up; and when thou hast opened his mouth, *thou shalt* find a piece of money; that take, and give unto them for me and thee." (Matthew 17:27 KJV, italics added)

"If ye then be not *able* to do that thing which is least, why take ye thought for the rest? Consider the lilies how they grow: they toil not, they spin not; and yet I say unto you, that Solomon in all his glory was not arrayed like one of these. If then God so clothe the grass, which is to day in the field, and to morrow is cast into the oven; how much more *will* he clothe you, O ye of little faith?" (Luke 12:26–28 KJV, italics added)

There are many verses showing that God is able, but I want you to look at one more verse, one that interested me far more than those that illustrated Jesus' abilities:

"Is this not the carpenter, the son of Mary, the brother of James, and Joses, and of Juda, and Simon? And are not his sisters here with us? And they were offended at him. But Jesus said unto them, A prophet is not without honour, but in his own country, and among his own kin, and in his own house. And *he could there do no mighty work*, save that he laid his hands upon a few sick folk, and healed them. And he marveled because of their unbelief. And he went round about the villages, teaching." (Mark 6:3–6 KJV, italics added)

Jesus was not able to perform miracles in this place because of the people's unbelief. The people there had known Jesus since he was a child and did not believe that he was able to do anything more than anyone else who they had watched grow up. Because they acknowledged that they did not believe that Jesus was able, he was not able to do anything, except heal a few sick folk.

While God is able to do all things, we stop his ability to bless our lives if we do not acknowledge that he is able (and maybe why your faith has not *worked*. You had not activated your faith). The verse did not say that he would not do mighty work there; being a testament of his will, but that he *could not* do mighty work there because of their unbelief. They acknowledged that Jesus was not able, in this verse, confirming again that the belief in his ability is the foundational seed of faith.

There are other possible misconceptions, hidden in plain sight, in this verse that brings some truth and understanding. This verse, as well as those that list the types of miracles we are allowed to request, tell us something about the miracle of being healed. It does not tell us, in this account, whether Jesus was able to heal the few sick folk who did not believe in his ability to bless their lives, or if the blessing of being healed is not as much a miracle as it is a blessing from our loving Savior. If he healed sick among those who did not believe that he was able, how much more is he willing to heal you from your disease or suffering, being a believer? In some way, however, those whom he healed would have used their agency so that Jesus would heal them. God cannot bless someone's life against their will, so there must have been some acknowledgment or request, even a pleading moan, for Jesus to heal some.

To move a little deeper so that we can more fully understand faith, why would Jesus ask everyone he healed if they believed he was able to do so? He did not do anything without purpose. It was not for self-glorification. He never asked for glory, always giving glory to his Father. Why did he require an acknowledgement? Why did he ask everyone he healed to acknowledge, verbally or through action, their belief that he is able to do whatever it was that they asked him to do? Never in any of the writings has God ever asked us to do anything that was unnecessary. Every ordinance, every prayer, every command is necessary to our own redemption, so to answer the question "Do you believe I am able to do this thing" must also be a necessary component of faith or Jesus would not have asked it.

Jesus asked of all he healed if they believed he was able because it was necessary for each of them to give an honest and insightful acknowledgment of their belief, to whatever level they believed. There is great power in the acknowledgment (testimony), of which we may not fully understand in this life and one that we have misunderstood, even forgotten, over the centuries. It was not for Jesus' sake that they had to acknowledge their belief, but for their own. Since Jesus did all things for our education, for this life and the life to come, usually pointing toward something needed in the life to come, it stands to reason that we may need to acknowledge that Jesus is able to save us at the final judgment. Remember that every tongue shall confess (an acknowledgment) that Jesus is Lord (Philippians 2:11 KJV). This declaration cannot be forced, but every soul will know, without doubt, to the point where they cannot help but acknowledge, that Jesus Christ is Lord and is able to save (we see that God will not lose the battle against sin because it will take an active rebellion to choose Satan, in the end—it will not be due to ignorance or misconception).

What we see, particularly in Mark (Mark 6:3–6 KJV), is that the acknowledgment that Jesus is able, activates a person's faith so that Jesus is *able* to heal them; because their acknowledgment that Jesus is *not able*, blocked his ability to do anything for them, except to heal a few who were ill. They may not have believed that Jesus was able, but they hoped that he could; probably due to their suffering. They hoped that Jesus was able, which allowed their healings. But, the other people's acknowledgements that Jesus was not able to do anything more than anyone else, were active rebellions, in their hearts; belligerent refusals against him. The rebellious acknowledgments inactivated their faith, by their agencies, and tied Jesus' hands. That means that it is a requirement for us to acknowledge, in some way, to stimulate or activate our faith. We first need the acknowledgement that Jesus is able for him to do anything for us, because of our agency.

There is one account that does not follow the pattern. There was a man who brought his son to Jesus to be healed but did not believe:

> "[But if thou *canst* do any thing, have compassion on us, and help us. Jesus said unto him, If thou *canst* believe, all things are possible to him that believeth. And straightway the father of the child cried out, and said with tears, Lord, I believe; help thou mine unbelief.] Bring him hither to me. And Jesus rebuked the devil; and he departed out of him: and the child was cured

from that very hour." (Matthew 17:14–17 KJV, italics added and bracketed text from Mark 9:22–24 KJV)

This man had dealt with his son's condition from childhood, which meant that his son was an adult. His son had great seizures that were frightening to witness. The son had thrown himself down onto the ground, foaming and gnashing his teeth, and becoming rigid, unable to move for some time. He threw himself into fire and into water many times to burn or drown him. I can only imagine that after all these years, this man felt utterly desperate to have his son healed and had exhausted all possibilities. Watching and caring for him for so long would have been more than he could bear—not that he was tired of caring for his son, but that it would be much more difficult since the son was a man and the father would be getting old. It is obvious that he was desperate, trying everything possible.

The man would not have brought his son to be healed if he had no hope that Jesus would be able to heal him, as others had claimed. He would have heard witnesses told by others who Jesus had healed, and perhaps even sought some of them so that he could hear the witnesses personally. It is clear that he hoped that Jesus would (will) do it for his son.

When Jesus asked him if he believed that he was able to heal his son, the man acknowledged his belief, and then did what many of us do when asked about what we actually believe: he second-guessed himself and then started to doubt, tearfully begging for help for his unbelief.

The request to "Help thou mine unbelief" illustrated that he had a powerful and firm desire to believe but he was unsure if Jesus actually could heal his son, probably because of the many other things that he had tried over the years. So, why did Jesus heal this man's son since he did not have the firm belief that he was able?

What does an honest and insightful acknowledgment do for a person that provides the necessary components to activate faith? As we have discussed before, there is power in the spoken word or we would not be judged by what we say. Since Jesus healed those who believed as well as those who doubted but hoped to believe that he was able, it is the honest acknowledgment of our belief that activates faith sufficient for a healing, or any other miracle, no matter where our belief is between hope and absolute knowledge. The honest acknowledgment, at whatever level (because of our firm hope and willingness to ask), is the use of our agency that gives access to Jesus' power, which immediately turns our hopes into faith once the Savior touches our lives. This is how Jesus was able to heal a few sick folks in a place that did not believe that he was able to do so. The honest acknowledgement of hope, or desire to know, allows it.

Just as we have discussed in the chapter, 'What is Faith?' we think that hope is a longing wish. This is not hope. Hope is the plan of action, done in faith; where a wish sits and waits for someone else to make that wish come true. The man took his son (the plan and action of faith) to Jesus with the hope (expectancy and trust) that he could heal him, not really believing that it was possible, but desiring so badly. He did not wait, wishing for something to happen. Likewise, the woman who had hemorrhaged for twelve years also illustrated hope when she first heard of Jesus' healings. Then when she learned that Jesus was coming to her town (because she would not have been able to walk very far, if at all), she devised the plan of faith to find a doorway in which she could crouch and await his passing. Then it was the hope turned to faith that propelled her arm to reach out and touch the hem of Jesus' robes, knowing that if she could even brush her hand on the fringe of his robe, she would be healed. Hope is an expectancy that something will happen rather than a wish that it would¾she hoped so much that she was willing to risk being trampled by all the people, in the square.

Faith is the completion of hope. The making of the plan of faith completes hope because it plans, moves, builds, and creates (action) from the anticipation of hope. Hope is the expectancy that we will gain salvation and a reward in heaven, while faith is the plan and action of obedience to the commandments of God and the repentance of our sins so that we may be found among those worthy (pleasurable and valuable in God's eyes) for such a reward—planning, obeying, listening, and doing, to ensure that we may receive.

The Bible does not require a specific level of faith, only a firm honest level. An honest acknowledgement of your belief makes it possible for you to hold a firm faith at any level because you do not need to hold something that you do not possess. It is simple and guarantees your success, and causes your faith to grow from its current level very quickly because you have experienced Jesus' touch in your life.

Now that you understand that you have a firm level of faith, no matter what level it is, by acknowledging your belief about Jesus' abilities, there is another hidden understanding that is necessary to activate your faith. Where the acknowledgement that God is able is the key, there is a substance that is necessary to fuel your vehicle of faith.

We discussed in the chapter, 'Worthiness,' that the desires of our hearts determine the direction we are facing on our life path, and it is our intents that fuel and propel our actions. Also, in the chapter, 'Ask and Ye Shall Receive,' we learned that we need to have heartfelt emotion, when we pray, or our prayers are only dead words. Talking about faith, it is our intent, our heart-felt desire, that causes the power in our faith. The man who brought his son to be healed, who did not quite believe but hoped, desired for his son to be healed. Those who were blind, lame, deaf, or had any other type of ailment had the desire to be healed. The woman who had the twelve-year hemorrhage, while it was her desire to be healed, it is this story that gives us a clue of the power of intention, which we cannot overlook.

When the woman who hemorrhaged for twelve years brushed against Jesus' robes, Jesus was startled and was stopped in his tracks. He told his disciple that power (virtue) had been taken from him. In that story, look at all the other people in the city that morning. There were hundreds of people who were pressing against Jesus, but there was only one woman plugged into his power, through faith. How sad it is to think that there was only one. They believed that he could bless their lives or they would not be there to see him (unless they were in the square in a similar way that we see a celebrity in our town) but really never understood who he was. Jesus was startled by this woman, crouching in a doorway, and noticed that there was one person among the crowd of people with the intention to be healed by him and had plugged her faith into his power.

There was a healing that I requested several times that led me to understand that we also need to have an element of intent in our acknowledgement, to propel our faith. Simply going through the motions and saying the words are not enough. The key of faith requires the intent in our hearts (emotions) to fuel our faith and plug into Jesus' power.

I had a strange headache on the left side of my head that could be felt around and halfway through my brain, directly in the center. It did not matter what I did, when I would do any activity that would raise my blood pressure (exercise, walk, climb stairs, laugh), I would experience an excruciatingly sharp stabbing pain in the same spot. An MRI and blood work showed nothing wrong but the pain continued each time my blood pressure increased. I started talking to Jesus about the pain and what it kept me from doing. I went through the motion to make sure that I had done everything correctly, but for several months nothing happened. I started thinking that I had received a 'no' answer, but that did not make sense since the Bible said that Jesus healed all who asked and he had healed my brain once before, not to mention other healings.

One day, I was editing this book when I read something that stopped me and started me to thinking. Immediately, I prayed and said my prayer again, pretty much as I had done before, but this time I engaged my heart and I immediately felt the healing fingers of my Savior, right in that spot. I have not experienced that pain again.

I thought again of the experience that I had that first day driving in my car, when Jesus healed the racing of my thoughts—my first healing. When I thought of my visualization, that morning, I realized that I had engaged my heart, intending, feeling the deep and strong desire to be healed. I realized that I had forgotten to communicate with my God and my Savior in the way that they communicate to me—through my heart.

We communicate (really communicate) with our Father like he communicates with us—using our minds (thoughts and words) and our hearts (emotions). This is the lesson from this healing—our faith devises the plan, our acknowledgment that God is able activates our faith, our words clarify the wanted desire, but the heart is what plugs our faith into Jesus' power.

Based on the information we have gathered, what we know about faith is:

- Faith is an active power.
- Faith centered in Jesus Christ may produce forgiveness, justification, purification, redemption, sanctification, salvation, and a reward in the life to come.
- To have faith is to have confidence in something or someone that is unseen or has not yet provided enough evidence or proof of its existence—in this case, Jesus Christ our Savior.
- Faith propels us to act on that which we place our faith, moving toward the fulfillment of tasks associated with that which we hold our faith.
- Faith must be based on truth and can be tested by using our spiritual barometer to see if it is simple enough for all to do successfully and equitably, allowing us to feel the love of God and Christ, and brings us closer to them without fear.
- Faith offers us the means to acquire the desires of our hearts and gives the ability to gain blessings from God; have the ability to do all things through Jesus by plugging into his power; be able to repent of our sins and be forgiven of them; and creates a personal witness of Jesus Christ through the Holy Ghost.
- Faith is developed as a natural consequence of personal righteousness, and must be cultivated and refined to align and realign our hearts' intents and desires to that of our Savior.
- Where there is true faith, there are miracles, visions, dreams, healings, revelation, and all the gifts of God; and since God is the same yesterday, today, and forever, they are available to those who live in this age, too.
- The effects of faith are that we know that our lives are acceptable to God and we have an assurance of our personal redemption through faith in Jesus Christ.
- Faith is the big bazooka of all weapons to combat evil, which amply battles, defeats, and protects its possessor from it—evil flees from those who have it.
- Faith must be activated by an honest acknowledgment of our belief that Jesus is able, at what level we believe, blended with the intent (emotions) of our hearts to fuel the faith and to allow us to plug into Jesus' power.

11

AN EFFECTUAL FERVENT PRAYER OF THE RIGHTEOUS

"The effectual fervent prayer of a righteous man availeth much."
(James 5:16 KJV)

Now that you have the foundational seed or key of faith firmly established, I hope that you have begun to ask for the blessings that you need and desire, or see that you will, very soon. While we have a couple of minor misconceptions left to correct, for the most part this chapter and the remaining chapters put all of your new understandings together and address questions that you may have trying and experimenting with it all, to gain results.

I know that the words *gain results* sound manipulative, but they really are not. The reason you picked up this book and have read to this point is because you badly want to receive results, and want your results to be more consistently than before. By understanding the foundational key of faith and how to pray in a way that God can answer you, you will receive the results you seek. It is promised many times throughout the pages of the Bible (ask, and ye shall receive).

Learning how to use faith to bring about miracles may feel like you are manipulating God to make things happen. These feelings are quite normal and quite human, and are what Satan wants you to believe so that you cease asking for and receiving blessings. He wants you to continue to be confused and frustrated, and gain misconceptions and false beliefs, and... feel like you did before you picked up this book.

While it feels like manipulation, it is very arrogant to think that we are capable of manipulating God. When put that way, we can see the truth. Because asking and receiving blessings strengthens and expands our faith in Jesus, and teaches us more about our Father in heaven and his Son than we could gain otherwise, we see that if we use our spiritual barometer, it clearly shows that asking and receiving blessings from God is a good thing, and so it is truth. God would not have given us tools and commanded us to use them if he did not want us to use them successfully.

In the Garden of Eden, God put a cherub and a flaming sword in front of the Tree of Life because he did not want Adam and Eve to partake of that tree after they had partaken of the Tree of the Knowledge of Good and Evil, thus being stuck in their sin with no possibility of release. So, if he did not want you to know this information, he would have prevented it from being written in the Holy Bible. He would have put angels to stop this information. God does not make mistakes.

God has given us tools to use. God is a god of order. It is essential to learn how to appropriately and successfully use these tools. It really is all about doing things correctly and according to what is written in the Bible. The way that we have attempted to use our faith to this point is chaotically and with a sense of desperation. That is not faith, nor can we hold any faith while feeling desperate, desperation being a form of fear. Remember that fear is the opposite of faith—the anti-faith.

When you begin using your faith, you may feel a little nervous. I know I did. I was taught that we are to wait for blessings from the Father, rather than to request them. It took me nearly a year to ask after I had been taught this information, and then it was because I lost my arch supports and I was in pain. Still, although I understood, in theory, that God wanted me to ask so that I may receive the blessings that he had in store for me, and I had learned the right way to ask so that God could answer me, I felt very uncomfortable—almost afraid. To ask for things, especially things that I considered to be miracles, being much larger in size than most blessings, in my mind, made me feel very uncomfortable and very selfish. On the other hand, the thing that I requested seemed silly and unimportant, certainly when compared to spiritual matters or death, life, and true suffering. I thought that my pain, while it was enough to keep me from walking, I considered it as unimportant—I mean, who asks for blessings from God on their feet because they lost their arch supports? I certainly thought my feelings were of no consequence.

Then the Spirit encouraged me to ask for that which I wanted, not only what I desperately needed (like I am encouraging you to do now, teaching you all that I would learn after this moment, which is that all righteous desires are available from God). Whatever it is that you think and feel, I urge you to take it to God in prayer. To plant a seed, you need to use it. In gardening, you never know if a seed is good until it sprouts, and you will never know if it will sprout until you plant and nurture it.

There is something that you desire from God. It may even be to know whether the things you have read here are true and are according to God's will. Pray. Ask, so that you may receive it. I urge you not only to take my words (I am another fallible human), but learning about this information and doing nothing with it gives you no benefit. Take it to God, to find out the truth of this information. Or perhaps you have a blessing that you have been thinking about, as you read these things, and want to ask. Ask. Do not let another day end without asking.

It is now the time to construct your effectual fervent prayer, using all of the information that you have learned. Because this information is so different, I will show you what my prayer would look like, asking to know if the information that you have read thus far is true (while I received this information from the Spirit, I do not presume that you should take my words without asking God—unless the Holy Ghost has been testifying of the truth of these things, as you read; which I experienced through the editing and publishing process). Feel free to use this as a pattern, changing any of the words to make it particular to you and your request. Please do not make this a memorized prayer, which would become ineffective over time. Memorized prayers do not hold the intent necessary to plug into Jesus' power. Use it only as a pattern until you gain the understanding that God will provide. Note that I will place brackets and upper case text to label the various components of your *Prayer of Faith*; and informational instructions in parentheses, as you pray:

"[PRAYER COMPONENTS] My loving and merciful Father in heaven, [DO IN JESUS' NAME] in the name of Jesus Christ I ask for help knowing your will about the things that I have read in this book. [PRESENTING THE INFORMATION] I have read here that a basic faith that is sufficient to bring about miracles in my life is a belief that you and Jesus are able to do all things. [ACTIVATION OF FAITH & SETTING FIRM BELIEF] Of course I believe that you and Jesus are able to do all things (adding what level your belief holds). I know that without doubt or question (or acknowledge the level you possess). [PRESENTATION, CONTINUED] I have read that I need to acknowledge my belief to activate my faith, as it shows in the Bible, so I am following these instructions to find out from you. [ENGAGING THE HEART] I so badly want to develop life-changing faith (feel this deeply and earnestly—engage your heart) and [PRESENTATION, CONTINUED] want to be able to ask for and receive blessings that my family and I need and want. I want to feel closer to you, and be taught and guided by you and your Son (feel this too); so I am experimenting by doing as this book suggests, for I can see how it follows what the Bible instructs, so that I may know the truth about these things. [ACTIVATION OF FAITH] I believe (at whatever level you believe) that you are able to do all things and so I know that you are able to let me know if the things I have read here are true and are according to your will. [ADDRESSING GOD'S WILL] I do not know if you will do this for me but I hope that you will. [SURRENDER TO GOD'S WILL] I surrender my will to you in this matter, and leave it up to you to decide if this is good for me to know.

"[PRESENTATION, CONTINUED] I have some concerns about the things I have read. They seem too simple to be true. It makes sense that you would make the requirements of faith simple enough for all people to do successfully, but I guess I wonder because it is something that is so different from all that I have learned before (change so that your concerns are applicable to you). [REQUEST OF BLESSING] I ask that you help me to know the truth. [DOUBLE-EDGED WISDOM STUPOR] If these things are true and according to your will, I ask that you remove all doubt, anxiety, concern, and any other fearful or worrisome emotions and thoughts from my heart and mind concerning them so that I no longer fear this information, and that they are made brighter, more brilliant, and very powerful in my heart, mind, and understanding; but if they are not in line with your ways and go against what you want for me to know and do, I ask that you remove the information from my heart and mind so that I am no longer affected by them. [ADDRESS DOUBLE-MINDEDNESS] I feel some fear about even asking you for this blessing, [USE AGENCY TO COUNTER] so please accept my words over any doubtful and fearful feelings or thoughts, or anything else, because I really want to know your will. Please allow my agency to override everything else that I may be feeling or thinking and accept my words over anything else.

"[WORSHIP GOD, PRESENTATION CONTINUED] I love you Father, and want to do your will in all things, and so I need to know your will about this information so that I do not become confused or stray from the path toward your Son. [REPENT AND ADDRESS UNREPENTED SINS] Please forgive me for any sins that may prevent me from receiving this blessing (repent of specific sins of which you are aware). I beg you to forgive me for all of my sins, so I may be closer to you and your Son (feel this intently). [ACKNOWLEDGING GOD'S PERFECTION & REQUEST TO KNOW WHAT IF NOTHING HAPPENS] I know that if nothing happens here that there is something of which I need to repent, or something that I have done wrong, because you are perfect and I know that the error is mine. If this is the case, please bring a clear and unmistakable recollection to my mind and heart of those things of which I need to repent, so I may repent appropriately; or clearly show me what I am doing wrong, by a bright and startling enlightenment to my mind, regarding it, so I may rectify it. [GRATITUDE] Thank you for the blessings you have blessed me with thus far (feel this), and thank you for your answer to my plea, here. I will patiently await your reply with gratitude and humility. Thank you, Father."

The prayer that I have written above is the full constructed Prayer of Faith (aka, effectual fervent prayer), addressing God's will, illustrating the *double-edged wisdom stupor*, and specifically requesting exactly how your wanted desire is experienced. The prayer also overrides the use of agency over any feelings or fears, preventing double-mindedness; addresses sins that may prevent the receipt of blessings; addresses gratitude; and starts the prayer in the name of Jesus Christ (which may be done either in the beginning or the end of the prayer). Notice that I also asked for very specific requests, asking for a *clear and mistakable recollection* if God sees that there are sins that require repentance, and *clearly show, by a bright and startling enlightenment,* the things that you may have done wrong, in that prayer, that may keep God from answering. All things for which we ask, requires that we specifically tell God how we want to receive them, because of our agency.

This prayer is also a great example of the type of prayer that will help you to ask for and receive blessings from God, removing a stupor if not needed. Requests for blessings usually do not need a stupor, but you can use one and then ask that if it is God's will that he give you the blessing as an answer to it.

In the chapter, "Ask and Ye Shall Receive," we discussed the components of requesting blessings. I will not detail these points again here, but will touch on them so that you have the total steps to construct your prayer of faith. Following these seven steps will help you to use the components to ask for blessings and finish your prayer. Focus on your desire, as you complete each one. If writing things down helps you, use that as a tool to prepare. God never said that we could not read our prepared prayers; he only does not receive those that are memorized and hold little or no feeling, in the heart:

1. **Consider you:**
    a. **Consider your desire.** Ensure that your request is a righteous desire. We learned that we need to ensure that our desire does not take anyone's agency, and that we do not do anything that is amiss. Think about what you are experiencing, specifically what you want and what you do not want, and what would be important for you to see, so that you know that it is by God's hand that you are blessed. This helps you to logically and specifically construct your prayer, getting it clear in your mind. Listing everything that you want will also help you to engage your heart, because you become more aware of exactly what it is that you want to experience.
    b. **Consider your belief** that God is able. In the chapter, 'Are You Able To Do This Thing?' we discussed that the foundational seed or key of faith is a belief that God is able to do that for which we request and is a question that Jesus asked to all those whom he healed. Acknowledging that God is able activates your faith and sets it at the firm level necessary for faith, at any level. Assess the firmness of your belief that God is able to grant your desire. Make it clear in your mind. Remember that it does not matter so much the level of your belief, but that you openly acknowledge your honest level of belief that Jesus is able, in your request. The power

is in the honest and open emotion-filled acknowledgment because you need to create a firm faith at whatever level you believe. It comes down to agency. Nothing can happen until you use your agency to acknowledge your honest level of belief that Jesus is able. When you do this, you plug your belief into Jesus' power, and then he is invested in making that thing happen.

c. **Consider your feelings.** Remember that God cannot answer us if we have any double-mindedness, so we need to assess and be ready to acknowledge everything that conflicts with our request (our words and emotions, etc). Consider any resistance, doubt, fear, anxiety, hesitation, etc., felt because it causes a conflict between the words we use to request the blessing from God, and the emotions and thoughts we experience, which God also reads. Write them down because you will need to acknowledge them in your prayer. Remember that double-mindedness is the biggest reason why many prayers are not answered. It ties Gods hands against you.

d. **Consider any unrepented sins.** There may be some sins that require repentance. We are unable to receive blessings while we are guilty of sin because they separate us from God and cannot favor us when we are still guilty. Ask for forgiveness for your sins and ask for a recollection of any that you may be unaware of, so that you may properly repent of them specifically, making sure to repent once you know. If you cannot remember any sins of which you need to repent, ask for God's forgiveness for your sins, anyway. God knows all, so he will know if you cannot remember any, but your willingness to repent (an act of agency) goes a long way toward being forgiven. Remember God said that he will forgive you of your sins once you repent of them.

2. **Construct your prayer of faith.** I have found that I use different types of prayers (or rather components of prayers) depending on their purpose: prayers of faith, wisdom or oblivion stupors, or

my normal prayers. I use my usual prayers if I am worshiping God, thanking him, or any other reason where I am not asking for anything from him. I use a prayer of faith when I request blessings, making sure that I am very specific; and I use stupors for requests for wisdom from God, so that I may know his will, without mistake; or to have something removed from me or someone else, like difficult temptation, anxiety, cravings, etc., or an appeasement, etc.

When you sit to construct your prayer, think about what kind of prayer that you need to construct. Then write your prayer so that you do not miss any necessary components. Writing it down helps the process clearer, in your mind. I wrote them down nearly every time, until I did not miss a step. To construct a prayer of faith:

a. **Detail your request.** Use powerful words, using those that are logical and which ensure that you engage your heart. Specify what you want your Father to do for you and the results of receiving your blessing, as if it was received exactly as you requested it.

b. **List any double-mindedness, and counter it.** Remember that the easiest way to do this is to counter it with your agency. You can counter any double-mindedness by requesting that your Father take your words over anything that you feel or think, explaining that you are using it through your agency.

c. **Address agency.** If your blessing is for you, specifying your desire will address your agency, but if it is for someone else, you need to ensure that you do not take away their agency. The easiest way to do this is to remove all requests of the other person to do anything, and then add language that allows their choice like, 'regardless to whether they choose to do it...,' or something similar.

This checklist of things to consider and address will help you to gain more success when using your faith to request blessings. It makes sense that we have different types of prayers for our different needs. God gave different sacrifices and offerings for different reasons and offences, so it makes sense to say different prayers for each purpose. You can add the different components of each prayer together once you have learned their different uses. It takes only a couple of times. Once you see the difference in your results, you will have it. Once you learn each component, you will move from prayer to prayer, component to component, smoothly. While I still typically use the various components of the prayers separately, sometimes I begin like I did as a child, thanking God for all my blessings; then ask for a stupor when I need wisdom; and then use the *Prayer of Faith* to ask for a blessing, all in the same prayer. You will learn to do this, too. For now, I want you to focus on learning the various uses of each type of prayer until you are able to do each one without writing them down. The Spirit taught me each component separately and I had to figure out what I could do with it. So, in the beginning, I want you to use each component separately before combining them to the same prayer. Remember that we are taught line upon line upon line and precept upon precept upon precept. Then you can write them combined, if you want to do so. Like everything else, we need to practice.

Before we move into the next chapter, I want to remind you to request blessings—lots of them. The only way to learn about our Father in heaven and Jesus is to work with them, learn from them, and gain wisdom from them. The only way to do this is to do all the things that come to your mind¾follow them. It is most likely that the tiny thoughts, in your mind, are the Spirit telling you to try it.

The things I learned most came from doing, experimenting, making a mess of it, and learning what I did wrong. Do not be afraid of mistakes. Mistakes are shortcuts toward gained wisdom, because they teach us more profoundly than any other way. These are your most important lessons. You are not required to be perfect. If nothing happens or you receive something that is not as you expected, ask God to help you to know the right way, so you can do it differently next time. Then listen to the promptings of the Spirit or thoughts that come in as wonderings. You need to practice to listen and recognize his voice, anyway. You cannot be too blessed from God. Ask, so that you may receive.

With these things firmly in mind, you are ready to take your first steps using life-changing faith, if you have not already done so. Prepare and make your request, so that you may know for yourself. Take the time today before you retire for the night. You will not learn the power of this information until and unless you test it. Any resistance is probably from Satan or his angels. Do not listen to him. If you are concern that it takes a great deal of time to pray in this way, take time early in the morning or late in the evening, when everyone else is asleep; or do it with another person, creating your respective prayers together. You have read this book thus far not only to gain information, but to gain understanding. You only gain understanding when you do what this information instructs. Remember that I did nothing with it for an entire year after I had been taught. Do not do like I did. I was foolish. Like everything else we learned thus far, it is simpler and easier than you expect, but you do need to practice a few times before you can do it quicker. You will learn to request blessings from God in this way by doing it. It only takes a couple of times. Do it now, so you can feel the awe and amazement that will follow.

"Wherefore by their fruits ye shall know them." (Matthew 7:20 KJV)

12

TESTED LIKE JOB

Knowing this, that the trying of your faith
worketh patience (aka, endurance)."
(James 1:3 KJV)

This is the chapter that most people would rather avoid. Thinking about having your faith tested conjures imaginations of horrors. Yet, the information that you have gained thus far has been easy to take, has it not—even exciting? It has helped you to feel closer to your Father in heaven and Jesus, and has caused you to feel more confident about developing and using your faith to bless you and your loved ones, right? Like all of the other misconceptions we have corrected (and this is the last one), you will find that having your faith tested is similar and far simpler than you expect, alleviating your fears, just like the others.

Now that you have begun your journey developing life-changing faith, because of all that you have learned and are doing to create an active and powerful faith, you should expect to have your faith tested (although you may not recognize it yet). Regardless of what you currently feel about tests of your faith, the thought may cause a great deal of fear. How will I be tested? What will I have to go through? Will it be painful? Will I and my loved ones suffer? Will I experience great loss?

Before I understood the truth about faith, the idea of having my faith tested was very frightening, to the point that I questioned whether I really wanted to develop faith. Thinking about tests of faith, I only thought of the story about Job (Job 1 KJV). I was afraid that any tests of my faith would be similar to his experience and I would lose everything I owned, lose everyone I loved, I would contract some horrifically painful and disgusting disease, and those I loved would mock me and tell me that I deserved it.

The story of Job frightens most people when they think about their faith being tested. Unfortunately, there are few other accounts in the Bible to make us feel better. Yet, the story of Job is another misconception about faith.

Job was a wealthy man who lived in a land called Uz. He had a large family and great wealth that comprised of seven thousand sheep, three thousand camels, five hundred oxen, five hundred female donkeys, and many servants. Job was greatly blessed from God because of his obedience to God's commandments.

According to the account, the sons of God presented themselves, Lucifer being among them. Conversing with God, Lucifer inquired about Job. Lucifer told him that he had protected Job and that if he stopped his protection, Job would surely curse him (the arrogance of the devil astounds me). So, God agreed to allow Lucifer to take away all with which he had blessed him. When this did not work out the way Lucifer had hoped, he went back to God and, knowing Job's heart, agreed that he could do anything to him except to take his life.

So, Lucifer killed all of Job's children, all of his oxen and donkeys, and killed all of his servants except the three that survived to report back to him of the three devastations. But even after all the destruction, Job did not curse God. Dedicated to force Job to curse God, Lucifer then struck Job himself with painful oozing boils all over his body and made him suffer with them for an entire year. Understanding Hebrew law, he would have been cast out of the city, like the woman who hemorrhaged for twelve years.

While Job's faith was indeed tested through all the horrific things that he went through, it was not really a test of his faith. Lucifer went after Job to break his resolve to serve God, and push him to suffer enough so that he would curse God. What Lucifer found, however, was that he could indeed break Job enough to curse the day he was born, but he could not force Job to curse God.

The conversation that Job had with his wife shows that this really was not a test of his faith: Job's wife, unable to watch her husband suffer any longer, told Job to "Curse God, and die" (remember that the Israelites, still in the wilderness, were killed each time people rebelled against God, striking them in some dramatic and tragic way; God had to teach them his law and the consequences for not obeying it. These lessons would have been still fresh in survivors' minds, and would have told the stories to younger generations), but Job came right back to her, asking "Shall we receive good at the hand of God, and shall we not receive evil?" He took the bad and the good without it affecting his resolve (many misinterpret what Job said to his wife, thinking that he said that God had given him the evil as well as the good, but that is not what it said at all. What he said is, 'Shall we receive the good at the hand of God, [comma—new subject] and shall we not also receive evil?' Job acknowledged that the good comes from God, but that he receives evil too from whomever or wherever it comes).

We also see others tested, in the Bible. While Abraham's test was a test of his faith, because the test was done by God, it was also a test to see if he was worthy to be the father of God's people and to be a prophet; and was instructed to serve only the true God, separating him from the Canaanites and their false gods, Molech and Ashtoreth, and their evil rituals.

Abraham lived in the land of Canaan. The Canaanites were a large nation of pagans, and so Abraham would have known and, possibly, worshiped their gods (see Joshua 24:2 KJV). Molech (aka: Baal) was the fire god, the god of the sun and the god of the underworld (hell). The idol was made of bronze that had a head of a bull and the body of a man. Usually, the idol had a fire pit into it, to which children were sacrificed by either throwing them into it, or placing them on its extended arms (also made of bronze), as an altar that heated up, burning them alive. Molech was worshiped by the Canaanites, the Egyptians, and the Philistines, among others (and all of the nations surrounding them), and was even adopted by the Roman Empire, before Christianity. Molech's mate was Ashtoreth (aka: Asherah), the goddess of fertility and war, the goddess of the moon and stars. Ashtoreth was also mentioned several times in the Old Testament. Rituals to Ashtoreth were done by sexual rites, sodomy and prostitution with the priests; and fortune telling, divinations, etc.

This is why God commanded Israel not to have anything to do with the people from these nations. Israel was drawn toward these practices because it was all that they knew, in Egypt; and it was all around them, after they left. There are many names for Molech, mentioned in the Old Testament. All mentions of a *false god*, in the whole of the Bible, referred to the worshipping of Molech and Ashtoreth. The worshipping of these idols was detailed in the Law of Moses. God abhorred these rituals, and commanded that Israel have nothing to do with them or the people who worship them.

Abraham was a righteous man. It does not state whether Abraham worshiped Molech and Ashtoreth, but is obvious that he was very familiar with its practices, because of God's command to sacrifice Isaac, Abraham's child. I suspect that he did not worship the idols, or God would not have guided and prompted him, as he did, and would not have chosen him as the father of his people. Instead, Abraham had learned to recognize the Spirit so well that he did not question, equally obvious that God was the only being whom he worshiped. When he heard the tiniest inkling in his heart that God may be speaking with him, he answered, "Behold, here I am" (Genesis 22 KJV). He would have received several previous tests of his faith because he had learned to recognize God's voice and kept a listening ear for him.

Thinking about Abraham's test of his faith, I imagine that in the still of the evening, Abraham went into his tent to rest from the day's work. Meditating, he felt the stirring in his heart. "Abraham," he heard God's voice in his mind. "Behold, here I am," he replied. "Take now thy son, thine only son Isaac, whom thou lovest, and get thee into the land of Moriah; and offer him there for a burnt offering upon one of the mountains which I will tell thee of," God commanded. This would have saddened him, but probably would not have shocked him, since children sacrifices were prevalent in that area. I can imagine that Abraham listened for more of the message, but there was no additional information to come, knowing the promises made to him, by God.

When Sarah came into the tent to retire for the night, Abraham pretended to be already asleep. Fortunately, she fell asleep quickly. As

Sarah fell asleep, he silently tip toed out of their tent. He begged God for a confirmation of the message, walking and talking to him through the night, but he did not receive one. Before dawn, he woke two of his servants to help him gathered the things necessary for the journey, and told a third servant that he was taking Isaac with him to sacrifice, so that Sarah did not worry. He did not want to wake Sarah and try to explain to her what God had commanded him to do, knowing that Sarah would not let her son leave, if he told her.

So, while Sarah was still asleep, Abraham took his son, Isaac, the two servants, and a donkey, and went toward Moriah—a three-day journey. Abraham was silent as they walked, cleaving to the bundle of wood for the altar. Abraham tried not to show his emotions. Each step would have filled with heartache, as he walked, remembering the promises that God had made to him, all those years ago, and the gift that he gave to his sweet wife, Sarah. Thinking about Sarah, Abraham questioned in his mind, "What would she say when I tell her what I have done? What would she *do*?"

The journey seemed to last a lifetime, but all the same, it seemed to go by too fast, getting closer and closer to the land that God had told him. He felt each breath break his heart, more the closer they got. On the third day, he could see the mountain. He asked his servants to stay in the trees, between the foothills, and wait for him and Isaac to worship privately, as they rested the donkey. Ironically, Abraham placed the wood bundle onto Isaac's back (just as Jesus would take upon himself the crossbeam of his own cross), took his knife and the lit torch, and they went, not saying a word.

Isaac watched his father as they walked, looking at him, the knife, and the lit torch, knowing that they would need a sacrifice for an offering. Finally, the boy's curiosity could not be silenced any longer. "My father," Isaac inquired. Abraham answered, "Here am I, my son." Isaac asked, "Behold the fire and the wood: but where is the lamb for a burnt offering?" Abraham's heart wrenched and he choked as he told his son that God would provide a lamb for the offering.

When they arrived to the place that God had told him, Abraham busied himself building the altar. He carefully laid the wood on top of the stones, as not to poke his son's body, fussing them about. He kept questioning how he would be able to do this thing, listening more closely for God to give him any other messages, questioning whether his God really requires sacrifices of children, too; and, importantly to him, ensuring to look in the opposite direction of Isaac so that his son did not see the tears streaming down his cheeks, as he worked. When Abraham finished building the altar, he turned to Isaac and looked at him, painfully yet lovingly.

Isaac was shocked to see his father's tears and tear-streaked cheeks through the dust on his face and wet stains on his robe. Abraham embraced his son tightly (uncomfortably tight), kissed him on the head several times, and bound him with strong cords. Isaac was alarmed and tried to ask his father what he was doing, but his father placed a finger over his lips, to silence him. He then placed his son onto the altar, binding him to it with more cords, so Isaac could not move. Isaac started crying from his fear and shock, questioning what his father was doing. Abraham, standing in front of the altar and sobbing, looked at his son's eyes for the last time. He took his knife from his sash and closed his eyes tightly. Tearfully and frighteningly, Isaac pleaded with his father not to do this thing. Abraham took a deep breath and looked toward the heavens, willing himself to surrender to what was commanded of him. Through his son's pleading cries, Abraham surrendered all of his will to God, and went to plunge the blade into his boy's chest, when an angel stayed his hand.

"Abraham! Abraham!" the angel shouted, loudly enough to shake Abraham's soul. "Here am I," he sobbed, trembling wildly. "Lay not thine hand upon the lad, neither do thou any thing unto him: for now I know that thou fearest God, seeing thou hast not withheld thy son, thine only son from me." Abraham gasped and opened his eyes, feeling his shock. He collapsed to the sand beneath him, letting go of the knife, sobbing, gasping, and quaking as the Spirit removed all feelings of fear and grief from him; and he could hear that the Spirit had given a stupor to Isaac, removing all memory of the incident from him, quieting him and causing him to fall into a deep sleep. Then the Spirit would have downloaded the command and clear understanding, into Abraham, to separate him from the Canaanites and their rituals, in that moment.

Still kneeling on his knees, hands into the sand to steady him,

Abraham was startled by a ram moving and rustling in a nearby thicket; his nervous system at high alarm from what he had just experienced. Wiping the tears from his face, Abraham feebly stood up, retrieved his fallen knife, and cut the cords from around his sleeping son, gently laying him in the nearby grasses. Cutting the ram that was stuck in the thorns, he bound him with cords and offered him up for an offering to God, in Isaac's stead.

Again, while Abraham was tested by God, being a test of his faith, this was an unusual test. Instead, we are mixing three things, thinking that they are all *tests of our faith*. You see, *life's trials*, *tests of our faith*, and *tests of our resolve* are three different things, yet they may run side by side and even intertwine. We may need to use the power of our faith while going through trials in our lives; and we definitely use faith when our resolve is tested, but these two are not *tests of our faith*. Trials are difficulties that occur in this imperfect life. We have difficulties that try us. While our resolve is our determination to serve God, our faith is the power, through Christ, that we may bring blessings to our lives and will ultimately save us from our sins. To understand tests of our faith it helps to see the distinct differences between the three.

I have had a test of my resolve to serve God and trust that he will help me through the darkest and most frightening time of my life. I have shared a little about this time, without going into specifics, for this time is still raw and I receive persecutions and judgments, although behind my back, regarding it. I went through the test of my resolve for just short of two years. I had made a horrible mistake due to betrayal, deceit, and my own failings. I lost all that I owned, my home, my job, my reputation—everything. Everyone who meant most to me hated me (with exception of my son and a few friends-turned family, angels really) and told me that I deserved it.

I remember the day, not yet a month after I was delivered from my test, when God whispered Job's name into my mind and heart, as I barely awoke one morning. That is all it was, the name "Job," but the feelings and understandings with which he flooded my heart were vast, humbling, awe-inspiring, and overwhelming, all at the same time. There was a deep and clear understanding that I came through my test as Job had, although I would not know what kind of a test I underwent until long after this moment.

Those who actively try to obey God, striving to do all that he may ask of him, may have their resolve tested in some way. Others may not be tested. For me, I wanted more. I always have. I wanted to know God and Jesus on a real and personal level. I deeply wanted to have experiences in my life like those in the Bible, and experience God's love for me that is empowering. I wanted to possess true understanding about spiritual matters—wisdom and knowledge. There is a price to be paid for those desires and obtaining them. I believe that evil seeks selfish and ignorant people, and puts it into their minds and emotions to target those who want more, trying to destroy those who want that type of relationship with God and Christ. Then there are others who neglectfully ignore what happens right in front of their eyes, thinking that anything said is dramatic, and so of no concern. Perhaps it sounds a bit melodramatic, but I do not think that the drama is too far from the truth—it was not, in my case.

Yet, the price paid for this type of test is so infinitesimally small, compared to the amazing knowledge, understanding, and blessings that God has in store for those who develop an absolute resolve to trust him through all circumstances and situations, it really does not compare. Losing nearly everything and everyone who meant anything to me is such a small price to pay to gain the small whisper of Job's name in my mind, and the vast feelings of pleasure and pride that God felt for me. I would go through it all again and again, and yet again, to gain the understanding, wisdom, knowledge, and tremendous loving feelings from my Father in heaven and Jesus that I gained. While I do not wish such a test on anyone, I do wish that everyone could feel as I did and gain the understanding from that morning. You will see each test as blessings in disguise, for the blessings that are given, after the test is over, are far sweeter than the difficulty of the test.

Building a personal relationship with God and his Son is awesome (in the true sense of the word). There is no superficial part of this relationship. You are taught things that help you, your family, and so many others around you. God will go before you, to make the journey through your test easier; and you will feel our Savior's presence with you, as if he is physically standing beside you at all times. You will feel his protection surround you, as if he is holding you in his cupped hands, protecting you from all harm and pain.

> "I will go before you, and make the crooked places straight: I will break in pieces the gates of bronze, and cut asunder the bars of iron: And I will give you the treasures of darkness, and hidden riches of secret places, that you may know that I, the LORD, who call you by your name, am the God of Israel." (Isaiah 45:2–3 KJV)

> "And the LORD, he it is that does go before you; he will be with you, he will not fail you, neither forsake you: fear not, neither be dismayed." (Deuteronomy 31:8 KJV)

You will experience the *treasures of darkness and hidden riches of secret places,* about which Isaiah speaks, the ability to stealthily do all that God requires, while others do not notice and do not hear. You will experience God's overwhelming love for you so greatly that you will not be able to handle its immensity, but all the same, you will not want the feelings to subside. The feelings are imprinted into your mind, your heart, and your cells that are truly unforgettable.

If you do go through a test of your resolve, please remember and look for the reality of these verses, for he will be with you, will not fail you, will not forsake you, and you will feel as if he is holding you in his very capable cupped hands. In that place, the only way that anything will frighten you is if you poke your head outside through the little triangular hole, made at the end of his thumbs, and look around (cup your hands with the length of your thumbs together on top of the two index fingers, and notice the triangular hole it creates at the end of the thumbs and pointed index fingers, as if praying). You will have to physically walk through the test, but you will only experience the pain and fright of it when you do not rest in him.

So, if *life's trials* and *tests of your resolve* are not *tests of your faith*, what is a *test of your faith*? Like everything else we have learned, a *test of your faith* is far simpler.

In the chapter, 'Are You Able To Do This Thing?,' we learned that there are three things that are required of our faith. Our faith must be (1) firm, (2) unwavering, and (3) unshakable. These three attributes must be tested. These are the tests of our faith.

Once you have requested something from our Father in heaven and have activated your faith by answering the question that Jesus asked of all those whom he healed, "Do you believe I am able to do this thing?" (acknowledging that you belief that Jesus is able at whatever level you believe), you have passed the first test of your faith (1–firm). *Firm* is simply a statement, an honest acknowledgement, of your belief.

In the chapter, 'Ask and Ye Shall Receive,' we learned that the acknowledgment of your belief that God is able produces a very firm belief, at whatever level you believe. Acknowledging that you believe that God is able at a higher level than you truly believe would create an instability in the *firm* test, and would cause the others to fail. In this test, you simply need to assess your honest level of belief to pass the test.

Once you acknowledge the firmness of your faith, your faith will need to be tested to see if it *wavers* from your human weaknesses. Most people usually second guess themselves, which may cause their beliefs to waver. This wavering can happen at any point after the initial acknowledgement.

After you acknowledge that Jesus is able, your emotions may cause your belief to destabilize and may waver if you hesitate, feel any fear about if God will bless you with your requested blessing, your worthiness for a blessing, whether you are asking for something that is amiss, etc. Usually, this wavering questions whether Jesus can really do that which you requested. It feels like an instability in your mind and heart. Yet holding your belief that Jesus is able, to whatever level you firmly believe, not allowing those questions and thoughts to make your belief waver from that firm level, re-acknowledging that Jesus is able, as necessary, passes the second test of your faith (2–unwavering). Separating all other things from your faith that God is able, focusing on *that* belief, stops any wavering thoughts and emotions (hint: basically, if you believe that Jesus is able, nothing else can cause it to destabilize because either he can do it or not, and your opinion does not change that).

In the beginning, through my tests of faith when I would feel my faith waver, I would say aloud whatever I was feeling or thinking, at the time, and then would add, "But I still know that Jesus is able to do this," sometimes said sarcastically, wondering if Satan was adding to some of them because some can be quite fierce. Acknowledging my feelings and adding that I still know that Jesus is able helped me to disciple my mind to focus on my firm level, keeping it unwavering from that level. Basically, it is a simple test to see if your emotions can cause your faith to waver from your firm level—but another acknowledgement that Jesus is able, answers it.

But there is a third requirement of faith that has not yet been addressed: our faith must also be unshakable. This third required test of your faith must be tested too, and the only way to do this is to see if it can be shaken.

> "And this word, Yet once more, signifieth the removing of those things that are shaken, as of things that are made, that those things which cannot be shaken may remain." (Hebrews 12:27 KJV)

The language in this verse may be tricky, but basically what it means is that those things that are shaken will be removed, while those things that cannot be shaken may remain. While this verse is actually talking about things (i.e., buildings or governments) that will be shaken and removed at Jesus' coming, it can also speak about other things, too. At the Second Coming, Jesus will shake the earth; however, not only objects that are shakable will be shaken to the ground and be removed, but shaky faith and belief in Jesus will be shaken to the ground and will be removed, as well, leaving only those whose faith is unshakable to remain. This is why we need to build our faith now, so we can learn and practice to be among those who will not be shaken at his coming. If you have learned to know Jesus, you will not be frightened by him.

I am sure that many are feeling some anxiety regarding this last test of your faith, but you have found that the first two tests were simple, so you will find the third one will be similar. Anything more than the other two tests (firm and unwavering), and it would not be a test of your faith. It has to be similar to the other tests. Tests of your faith should never cause you to lose or reduce your faith, but only strengthen it and help you to recognize the voice of the Spirit when he speaks. This test only tests to see if your faith can be shaken off that firm level, so you can learn how to make it unshakable.

We received a synopsis of Jesus' tests of his faith in the Bible. These verses detail the simplicity of having our faith tested. Jesus' tests of his faith were recorded in Matthew 4, and Luke 4. Jesus was tested with and passed very simple tests. Looking and pondering on these chapters, we may gain some insight. I remind you again that for him to be the perfect example his tests would be similar to ours; and because both Matthew and Luke recorded this account, this means that Jesus' tests were significant and we should fully understand the information it contains, although hidden. So, what understanding can we gain from Jesus' tests?

Jesus was tested by the adversary, showing that his resolve was tested. Evil tests our resolve, trying to break it and turn us away from Jesus; but God tests our faith because it is for the purpose of strengthening it. Satan could not or would not do anything to strengthen someone's faith, but because Jesus was a God and had perfect faith, he did not need his faith strengthened. Yet, someone had to test Jesus' faith in order to give us the prime example, and because his Father would have been viewed as a partial tester, Satan was allowed to test his faith and his resolve, trying to break them and, essentially, break *him*, which a test of resolve does. Jesus is the only person that God allowed Satan to test his faith because of his Godhood. It is important to understand that Jesus had not yet become perfected, in this life. He had the ability to sin, being part human, but only had the wisdom, judgment, and ability not to. For his example to be perfect for us, he would have to be imperfect to be equitable, compared to us humans. If he was perfect, his example would have been of no value (see Matthew 5:48—if he was perfect, he would have referenced himself, not his Father, who *is* perfect). Then to make it even more difficult, Satan used all of his trickery to add temptation onto his other tests.

To see the tests of Jesus' faith, we need to separate the three tests. Let us look first at his temptations. How could Jesus be tempted?

What could the devil use to tempt the God of the universe? Jesus was tempted with the same things that the devil uses to tempt us. To be an example for us, he must be tempted by the same types of things that would entice us.

Jesus was extremely hungry and quite weak after fasting for forty days and forty nights (the number does not necessarily mean forty. Hebrew numbers are more symbols than numbers, but it would have been a significant number of days), so Satan tempted him with bodily appetites—food: "Command that these stones be made bread." Jesus replied, "it is written, man shall not live by bread alone, but by every word that proceedeth out of the mouth of God" (Matthew 4:3–4 KJV, Luke 4:3–4 KJV).

Then, Satan tempted him with his life, his witness, and his power. Taking Jesus to the pinnacle of the temple, especially in his fatigue, would be similar to holding a pistol to someone's head and forcing them to deny their testimony; plus using spiritual power when it was not prompted, is a sin. On the pinnacle of the temple, Satan "saith unto him, If thou be the Son of God, cast thyself down: for it is written, he shall give his angels charge concerning thee: and in their hands they shall bear thee up, lest at any time thou dash thy foot against a stone." Jesus knew who he was, and simply replies, "Thou shalt not tempt the Lord thy God" (Matthew 4:5–7 KJV, Luke 4:5–8 KJV).

So then "the devil taketh him up into an exceeding high mountain, and sheweth him all the kingdoms of the world, and the glory of them; And saith unto him, All these things will I give thee, if thou wilt fall down and worship me." Since the others did not work, Satan tempted him with greed and blasphemy. It sounds to me that Jesus was annoyed by Satan, at that point, for he simply cast him away: "Then saith Jesus unto him, Get thee hence, Satan: for it is written, Thou shalt worship the Lord thy God, and him only shalt thou serve" (Matthew 4:8–10 KJV, Luke 4:9–12 KJV).

We see Jesus' temptations in the categories of things with which Satan tempted Jesus. We see that Satan tempted Jesus with the same things that he tempts us (bodily appetites, denial of our testimony, greed, glory, riches, blasphemy, etc.).

We see Jesus' test of his resolve in the feelings of the devil's demands (change these stones into bread, cast yourself down off the pinnacle, and worship me and I will give you the riches of the world). We see that the devil tried to make Jesus forget that he is the Son of God, asking him that '*if* you are really the Son of God...,' demanding that he accept anything else. Although the record does not indicate it, the test would have made Jesus forget who he was, which is Satan's favorite trick, making him feel bad about himself and putting him through emotional hell, because this is what a test of resolve does. Satan tries to destroy your resolve to obey God, trying to create a rebellion against him by making you forget all that God has done for you, and that you are precious to him, trying to break your spirit. If Satan can get him to fear or think badly about himself, he can break him (honestly, I think that they only reason why I did not break completely was because Jesus was very present with me the entire time, and he had ask me to spend that time as a mission for him. By the end of my test of my resolve, I was pretty broken but my resolve was not broken).

You see the account of Jesus' tests of his faith when you remove all evidence of the tests of his resolve and the temptations. Removing what Satan demanded, which I admit is most of it, and focusing on what Jesus *said*, albeit abstract, you see the same three acknowledgements to achieve the firm, unwavering, unshakable faith: one to set his belief firm, one to keep his emotions from wavering, and a re-acknowledgment to ensure that his belief is unshakable.

Just like the other two tests of faith, firm and unwavering, the third test simply needs another acknowledgment of that firm level of faith. This is also what Jesus did during the tests of his faith. He acknowledged his belief, his truth. Jesus firmly acknowledged that he is the Son of God with his words: "It is said...," talking about all prophecies regarding him, establishing his firm level of faith in himself, as they Messiah. Then when Satan took Jesus upon a pinnacle, in his fatigue, to try to force him to fear—his favorite tool—Jesus unwaveringly acknowledged that he is the Lord, with the words, "thou shalt not tempt the Lord thy God," answering the second test of his faith. Then when Satan tempted him with the world's riches, glory, and blasphemy, he unshakably acknowledged that he is the Messiah, with his words, "it is written, thou shalt worship the Lord thy God, and him only shalt thou serve"; and then he showed that he was able when he cast Satan out of his presence. Three acknowledgements at that firm level, giving us the perfect example of how to win against evil, every time.

Many of those who I have explained that three simple re-acknowledgments of your belief that God is able answers the three tests of our faith did not believe me. It has to be bigger. It has to be scarier. It has to be painful..., right? No. It does not. If it did, it would not be a test of your *faith*. I will repeat it again. Tests of your faith simply *tests your faith*, it does not try to destroy it.

Once you activate your faith by establishing a firm level by acknowledging that Jesus is able, in your initial request, you need to keep your faith from wavering from that firm level. Your emotions cause tempests in your mind and your heart (and your faith) that make them waver. You see what the tempest did to Jesus' disciples, in the sea. This is what this story was teaching us, but you do what Jesus did when he awoke. You stand up and calm the turmoil within and around you, and simply re-acknowledge your belief that Jesus is able. Then God tests your faith to see if it can be shaken from that firm level. In this test you experience little thoughts, feelings, or sensations regarding the faith you just used. These tests will make you question whether Jesus really is able to do what you asked. During this test, you will feel small symptoms (pain, illness, etc.) of the thing you requested, to see if your faith can be shaken and crumble from its firm level¾to see if you truly believe that Jesus is able. But all you need to do is to re-acknowledge that Jesus is able, each time when you experience the symptoms. This is key.

Are these true tests of our faith? These simple tests are true tests of our faith because it is not as easy as it sounds, although it is not difficult either. It just takes discipline. The Spirit is an excellent teacher. Once you realize what is going on, you will learn to struggle a little until you have the faith that is firm, unwavering, and unshakable. It only takes a few times. It has to do with disciplining your mind and emotions to focus on Jesus' ability to save; and it is exactly what it is doing. These tests make sense because everything points toward Jesus' ability to save us.

There is a clue that Mark records Jesus teaching us, which helps us to ensure that we pass the tests of our faith every time.

"And Jesus answering saith unto them, Have faith in God. For verily I say unto you, That whosoever shall say unto this mountain, Be thou removed, and be thou cast into the sea; and *shall not doubt in his heart*, but shall believe that those things which he saith shall come to pass, he shall have whatsoever he saith. Therefore I say unto you, What things soever ye desire, when ye pray, believe that ye receive them, and ye shall have them." (Mark 11:22-24 KJV, Italics added)

Jesus specified where doubt (the wavering or shaking of our faith) occurs: they occur in the heart. Understanding this makes the passing of the tests of our faith much easier. Because doubt happens in the heart, it does not matter much that we have wild thoughts running through our minds, during tests of our faith. Jesus told us that the wild thoughts, in our minds, are not doubts. Because we understand that doubt happens in the heart, we only need to keep the wild thoughts from questioning whether we truly understand and believe that Jesus is able. This is why it is beneficial to say aloud whatever we are thinking about, *and* then state again that we still know that Jesus is able. We can allow the thoughts to run through our minds, keeping our hearts stable, thus passing all tests of our faith easily. Knowing that doubt happens in the heart, and not in our minds, means that countering any double-mindedness with our agency is the easiest way to pass these tests. It does not matter that thoughts may be wild, thinking about if God will bless us with the blessing we have requested. It does not matter about anything that our thoughts take us. These thoughts are simply part of the test. Asking that our words are accepted over our hearts and minds, and acknowledging that we know that Jesus is able, is the easiest way to pass these tests, thereby making us more successfully ask for blessings from God, and receive them.

Jesus gave us another tool that we can use, especially when we experience evil or fierce temptation. When Jesus acknowledged his third acknowledgement, he turned to Satan and casted him from his presence. Because Jesus did all things for our example, we are able to use Jesus' name to cast Satan and his angels from us, too. We see that Jesus cast

Satan with the words, "Get the hence, Satan for it is written, Thou shalt worship the Lord thy God, and him only shalt thou serve." This means that for us, we can say, "In the name of Jesus Christ, I command you, Satan and his angels, to depart," acknowledging our belief that Jesus is able, knowing that we are able to do this because this acknowledgement plugs our faith into Jesus' power.

Tests to our faith have all the following six characteristics:

1. Tests of our faith are done by our loving Father in heaven, not by evil forces. Evil tests our resolve because it tries to destroy it, but God only allows those people who are able to pass a test of their resolve to go through one, knowing their hearts. God will never allow someone who may not survive from a test of their resolve to go through one because it would not serve his purposes, gambling with their resolve to serve Jesus.

    No evil will come to you when your faith is tested because it would cause confusion, and God would not allow confusion to occur, especially during this time. In fact, I have never experienced anything negative when my faith was being tested. If you experience anything negative at all, it may be within your own doubt, where you simply acknowledge these doubts honestly to God and tell him what you want to have happen: "I would like to have an unwavering faith, without doubt. I know that you are able to do all things, however, and know that without any doubt," or use your agency: "I choose to believe".

2. Tests of our faith feel exactly like promptings from the Spirit— whispers or wonderings— but the feelings make you wonder if God is *testing* you. If you wonder if God is testing you, accept that he is and look for the symptoms of the tests and simply acknowledge and re-acknowledge that you believe that Jesus is able.

    Just when you are receiving a message from God (a prompting), notice the tiny feelings of urgency with the tiniest thoughts, in the back of your mind, or those that come up unexpectedly. These feelings of urgency with the thought wondering if God is testing you may help you to recognize it (part of the test is recognizing God's voice, when he speaks).

These small feelings of wonder and urgency, with a tiny thought, tell you something. Listen to it. This is the voice of the Holy Spirit. Do not discount it. It is smaller than you anticipate but it is noticeable and the message gives you a clue what it is about. Listen to what it is telling you. Feel the feelings. Remember that God does not do anything that causes confusion, for confusion is not of God. If you wonder if you are being tested, simply accept that you are, so that you do not miss the test and receive the knowledge or reward for it. I cannot say this enough.

3. Tests of our faith will not be painful, tragic, scary, or cause loss. Pain cannot cause an increase of faith. Tests of our faith are supposed to increase and perfect our faith, not cause fear or destroy it—it cannot because fear is the opposite of faith. Throughout Jesus' journey, he never illustrated anything frightening, disastrous, terrible, or any type of loss. Instead, he showed us an example of peace, love, faith, and ability. During Jesus' tests, he did not experience pain, loss, or catastrophe, but simply acknowledged his truth throughout. As the perfect example, we see that tests of our faith cannot hold pain or loss.

4. Tests of our faith will be instantaneous; they will only last long enough to think about it and re-acknowledge your firm belief to show that it does not waver or cannot be shaken. In the story about Job, his test was ongoing for about a year. This was not a test of his faith. Likewise, my test of my resolve lasted for just shy of two years, showing that mine was not a test of my faith, either. Learning about tests of our faith, after my test of my resolve, showed me that the two tests are very different.

    Your faith can be tested multiple times for the same request through the course of the healing process, for example, to make sure that your faith cannot be shaken. It is not, however, a constant test. Also, *unshakable* is the only level that I have experienced that can occur multiple times. *Firm*, of course, is only once to set the level of belief, but *unwavering* was only done one time, each time, too. *Unshakable* was the only level of any of my tests of my faith that was done multiple times for the same thing, to see if it can be shaken from its firm level. This is a good thing to remember.

In another set of tests, I started to feel the nerve pain down my arms to see if my faith could be shaken, knowing that I had received a healing to my nerve pain earlier. I re-acknowledged that I knew that God was able and it fizzled out.

5. Tests of our faith have something to do with the use of your faith, and will not change. In the story about Job, his resolve was tested by losing his children, his servants, his animals, his crops, and then by getting boils on his body. None of these had anything to do with a request for blessings or the use of his faith. Likewise, the test of my resolve had nothing to do with the use of my faith. The test of your faith is directly related to the use of your faith so that you can learn to hold it firmly, unwaveringly, and unshakably under the most difficult of circumstances.

Tests of your faith must directly relate to the use of your faith, otherwise it would cause confusion. To be tested on something that does not directly relate to what you know, is like asking a first grader to take a MSAT (Medical Scholastic Aptitude Test). Not only would the child never understand the questions but they would not have the information to come up with an answer. The only way that a true test is given is that the pupil is taught the information, given some real-life applications that gives the student some context, and then tested to ensure that the questions, as well as the answers, are understood, and this is what God does for us. For your test of your faith to be tested, the test has to be something regarding the faith that you just used, or you would not know it was a test of your faith and you would be confused. God does not trick anyone.

As you begin the tests of your faith, they will start with small things. But as your faith becomes more powerful, your tests will be larger, too; like testing my faith with my fears of beetles. God will test your faith to deal with your fears and phobias, to rid you of them, because fears are evil. He will help you trust Jesus as he does, helping you to do specific things to rid you of the fear.

Then, as you continue growing in your faith, you may be commanded to do things in order to receive those larger blessings, or to take you to a new level of understanding, wisdom, and ability, in your faith. The types of things always serve to perfect you in some way to make you more like Jesus.

Because I had asked God to protect me from beetles, I had several different tests regarding bed bugs (fun!). One time, there was the tiniest thought in my mind that questioned if I trusted Jesus. "Of course, I trust Jesus," I thought. "Well, then why are you still worried about seeing bed bugs?" I did not hear a voice, only a tiny thought. So, every time I went into the bathroom for a while, I said to both of us (me and Jesus) that I believed him, and I tried very hard not to look around to inspect for any critters, not that I had found any, other than the chastisements I received about two years earlier. A couple of weeks later, I awoke to find one very itchy bite on my arm. I panicked. I felt the smallest wondering that I was being tested, and I remembered that I had heard a buzzing in my ear as I dozed off to sleep, the night before. Bed bugs do not buzz, and I realized that there must have been a mosquito in my bedroom. I focused on the wondering tugging that I felt and noticed that God was testing me, so I calmed down and said again that I trusted Jesus and that I knew that he is able to protect my apartment from beetles. The next morning, I noticed another very itchy bite on my other arm in nearly the same place. I panicked again and walked toward the apartment's property manager's office to show him. While the *wondering* was not any louder, the urgency was. I remembered the buzzing in my apartment the previous night, too, and so I calmed myself down and said that I trust Jesus again, acknowledging that Jesus is able to protect my apartment, returning back to my apartment without going to the office. Interestingly, the bites disappeared immediately when I remembered the buzzing and turned back toward my apartment.

While I think I failed most of those tests, they served to discipline my trust and faith. This is what Jesus does in your tests of faith. Your education will be very personal and very loving, and you will be led by him.

6. To pass the test, you simply re-acknowledge that you believe that Jesus is able, do what is commanded, and/or struggle with your human nature, as God commands. Most of the time, you simply need to re-acknowledge your level of faith (the same firm level of belief that God is able), to whatever that level is, to show that your belief does not waver or cannot be shaken from that level. There is no requirement of unwavering-*er* or unshakable-*er* belief—your faith does not need to be increased on a test; it only needs to be kept from wavering and shaking from its current level. Be sure that your belief that God is able does not waver by worries about God's willingness, your worthiness, or any emotion or thought that can cause you to waver or shake. If you feel like you may start to shake, tell God that you *choose* to continue to believe, using your agency, for as long as it takes (unshakable—a good use of stubbornness); or acknowledge that your faith is shaking and ask "Help thou my unbelief," which is a tool that you can use.

Sometimes, especially as your faith grows, God may require you to do something, as a test of your faith. Just do it. Most of the time it is best to do it without thinking about it. Just make sure that you learn to recognize the voice of the Spirit when God tests your faith. Ignoring your tests gives you a failing grade and gives you no benefit. Your faith can only grow as you pass each test of your faith.

You may be asking what does this do to your faith. It is too small, too significant for this to be a test of your faith, right? No. This is powerful—simply powerful! I look at these tests of our faith like an infant learns to walk. Looking at it this way is far more accurate for us to see it from our adult perspective. Because all of us must be able to have our faith tested, ensuring equity, the tests must be simple for all to be able to do successfully. We learn to have powerful faith not by starting with powerful faith, but by starting with small faith and small things, growing with each test, until it is very powerful and unflinching. But if you did not pass your tests because you either did not recognize them as tests, did not recognize the voice of the Spirit, or you did not know that you needed to be tested, your faith would not grow, being stuck at that level. Are you seeing why your faith was stuck before you learned about faith? Fascinating, isn't it?

Remember that tests of your faith may be a prerequisite to receive the blessings of which you just requested. Watch for the possibility of the tests and follow them. Look for the possibility of tests of your faith. You do not want to miss them because, after you are tested, is when you either receive the blessing or are given the understanding and wisdom from the lesson. In any case, you are taken to the next level of your faith, understanding all that you have learned at that level. You would not have received any of it if you had not passed the tests of your faith, due to neglect, not noticing, or not knowing that you need to do it. This is key.

Testing your faith to ensure that it does not waver or be shaken from its firm level is really the point of your faith when Jesus comes again. Going through my own tests of my faith and the test of my resolve, and experiencing it all, I am convinced that we will have to acknowledge that Jesus is able in order for him to save us, in the end. Plus, if we have had our faith tested, we will recognize him when we see and feel him. It is all about Jesus.

13

FREQUENTLY ASKED QUESTIONS

> "Wisdom is the principle thing: therefore get wisdom;
> and with all thy getting get understanding.
> (Proverbs 4:7 KJV)

This chapter is not to teach, but to fine tune your knowledge, and answer questions about things that may have gone wrong, as you experiment on your new tools. Because our God is a god of order, it is our responsibility to learn to do things the way he wants us to do it, so that he may answer our prayers. This chapter is not your only resource. The Spirit is there to teach you and guide you to all truth. If you have not started experimenting with the information here, it is time to do so. The Spirit will lead you. Experimentation helps you to learn about faith far quicker than simply reading about someone else's experiences. God wants you to learn about faith, and the only way to truly learn is to experiment.

> "Howbeit when he, the Spirit of truth, is come, he will guide you into all truth: for he shall not speak of himself; but whatsoever he shall hear, that shall he speak: and he will shew you things to come. He shall glorify me: for he shall receive of mine, and shall shew it unto you. All things that the Father hath are mine: therefore said I, that he shall take of mine, and shall shew it unto you" (John 16:13–15 KJV).

God will teach you in his own wonderful way, now that you have knocked on this door. Ask for guidance to know what you have done wrong. Continue reading, for I will answer many of the questions that may arise.

While I will not know your results, I know that while I experimented from all that I had been taught, I made many mistakes. I know that I have said it a few times before, but I want you to start working with these tools, unlike I did—I waited for an entire year before I started using them. I like to think that perhaps I needed to fail each time to gain the wisdom of my errors so that I could write this part of the book (at least thinking this way makes me feel better). I know that wisdom comes by making a mess of things, making horrible mistakes, and figuring out how to make it right at some point; struggling to learn, listen, and change. There are some things that you need to keep in mind as you experiment. These things may be small errors that keep you from obtaining requested blessings. Review these very carefully. I will address each issue and offer solutions to counter them. I will use many more of my own experiences in this section, rather than biblical examples and verses, so that you may learn from my mistakes and victories.

Hopefully, this section may serve to be a go-to section whereby you can hone your skills in developing and using life-changing faith. This chapter will also illustrate what happens once you have developed life-changing faith, the things that I have learned since my education from the Spirit, so you can see that our Savior continues to teach you. Our education is a lifelong endeavor—a wonderful journey.

This education, for me, came over the course of about a year and continues. The beginning and the most complex part of your education is to learn to hear and recognize the voice of the Spirit. Learning to hear and recognize the voice of the Spirit is not hard. It only needs a little practice and finesse¾recognize the possibility that God is communicating with you, and the courage to follow through to his instructions, as if you realized that it was a prompting. Jesus is there to help you through each step as you hone your spiritual skills. Do not be afraid to make a mistake. Just keep trying, and stay willing to continue. You gain wisdom with every misstep. Then you try again and succeed. The Holy Ghost, your guide, is very patient.

I have had several questions about developing life-changing faith. I will try to answer them in the clearest way possible.

How specific do I need to ask?

(Review the chapters, 'The Power to Choose Our Desires' and 'Ask and Ye Shall Receive.') Because our agency is of utmost importance to God, he is unable to bless you unless and until you are very specific about what you want to experience in your requested blessing. Be as detailed as you are able, thinking through it completely, from beginning to end, to see possible effects that you may not consider. By asking specifically what you want, detailing exactly how you want it experienced, you receive far more miraculous results, and since you have detailed your desired results, you will know that it is by God's hand that you have been blessed.

I was born with high arches. My arches were so high that my feet did not quite sit in my shoes except on the balls and heels of my feet. In my teen years, I nearly constantly wore three- to four-inch high heels. I worked at a bank for eight hours and then managed a men's department, at a department store, for eight hours on the weekdays, and then worked eight hours on Saturdays. Then I usually went dancing after work two to three times per week with a friend. Because of my high-heel shoes, my arches ended up folding in the center of my arch, folding my foot in half. Later, because of the length at which I wore them, I had to wear boy's heavy leather Buster Brown® shoes (these were the only shoes with enough room for my rigid high arch supports and my foot). If I did not wear my arch supports, my arches would sag and send severe pain through the most of my body. When I lost my custom-made arch supports during a move and could not afford to get another pair, I was in so much pain that I decided to ask for a healing of my feet.

This was my first request for a healing since I accidentally stumbled across the key of faith (a year later), so this was my first experiment with the information I had been taught. I asked God to heal my arches. I thought my request was specific because I asked for the specific parts of my body that I wanted healed, but when nothing happened, I turned to the Bible to figure out what I had done wrong¾at least I was wise enough to realize that the error was mine and not God neglecting to answer my prayer. During my daily Bible studies, that day, I found the story of Abraham's servant's prayer, when he was sent to look for a wife for Isaac. I saw how very specific his request was. He requested even for specific words to be said so that he would know for sure which woman was chosen.

I thought about how I wanted my feet to be but did not know anything other than what I had already experienced. I went back to God in prayer and asked that he bring my feet back to where they were when I was a child, before I damaged them by wearing the high heels shoes, with exception to the bones that were repaired through surgery¾I made sure to include this in my prayer because I did not want to have that problem return. I thought about the pain that moving the bones back should cause and I told him that I was willing to go through any pain that was necessary for this healing. I told him that I knew that he was able to do all things and so I knew that he was able to do this. The pain I experienced was sufficient to engage my heart, as I explained all that I felt.

The next day, the pain in my feet, legs, and back were gone, and I have not had any since. It took a few months for the deep folds in the center of my arch to smooth out, but they were significantly lower, back to the place where they were when I was a child (and I did not experience through the healing).

The reason God requires that your request be very specific is so that he is able to answer your prayer, and to ensure that you know that it was by God's hand that you were blessed. There is no reason for him to bless your life unless it strengthens and grows your faith in Jesus, so to bless you and not be able to understand that it was God who blessed you, is pointless. All things point to Jesus. I say this over and over again so that you deeply understand. ALL things point to Jesus. EVERYTHING good is about Jesus. It is ALL about Jesus and his ability to save us. Satan also knows that everything points back to Jesus; that is why he tries to make us look everywhere else, except him.

It is essential that you word your request very specifically, explaining God exactly how you want to experience, even down to the exceptions¾the bones that had been repaired during surgery. In my first attempt, I asked for my feet to be healed, but did not request how I wanted them healed. I only received the blessing after I explained exactly how I wanted them to be—to have them back to the way they were when I was a child. I had choices. I could have requested completely flat feet, although I have heard that there are some problems with them too. I could have asked for my arches to be lowered, explaining how far. I could have requested that they be like someone else's feet. I think I could have even diagramed them in the exact way I wanted them and it would have been done that way. There were many things I could have asked for, but I did not know how any of them would have felt, so I simply asked for my feet to be put back to the way they were when I was a child, with exception to the bones that had been fixed surgically. Because of my agency, God was only able to bless me when I specifically told him how I wanted my feet to be.

Using your agency to request a specific blessing brings more success to the receipt of that blessing, and like Abraham's servant, you will know that the blessing is from God, which further increases your faith.

Be very careful with the words you use in your request. "*Can* you help me?" is a question that illustrates that you do not believe that he is able (can). "*Will* you help me?" is a better choice of words. While you mean the same thing, your words count. Your words illustrate your agency. To acknowledge "I know you are able but will you?" is an even better choice and will bring about miracles, if you detail what you want clearly and specifically because these words separate the firmness of your belief that God is able and acknowledges that his will is his alone.

Will I be asked to do anything more?

Part of God's will is God's requirements. We ask for blessings, specifying our wanted results, and leave the rest to his infinite wisdom. God may require something from us to receive the blessing. Part of our responsibility is to follow through with what God requires, doing it completely.

Several years ago, my late husband received a diagnosis of CML (Chronic Myelogenous Leukemia). Right after his diagnosis, he spent twelve days at a local cancer hospital. While he felt much stronger than he did when he went into the hospital, he was still very weak when he was released. His appetite began to reduce to the point where he did not want to eat at all, and he got weaker, despite the medications. He requested a healing blessing, so we prayed the *Prayer of Faith*. After our request, I was prompted to purchase a machine that would blend fresh organic fruits and vegetables to make a smoothie in the morning and soup in the afternoon. This would basically predigest his meals for him so his body would absorb the nutrients without the effort of chewing and digesting. After two weeks of the daily smoothies and soups, his blood levels stabilized, he began to quickly feel better and stronger, and his cancer labs showed that he was beating the cancer. But after eating the smoothies and soups every day for several months, he stopped taking them because he was tired of the taste of fresh fruits and vegetables. Within only a few weeks, his blood levels destabilized and he ended up needing chemotherapy infusions. He received promptings telling him to get back on the nutritional smoothies and soups, but he did not do what he was prompted to do and ended losing his life to the disease.

We asked for a healing. Did he receive a healing blessing, or not? Many times we receive a blessing that requires some things for us to do. There were many healings that Jesus did that required the recipient to do or not do something ("Wash in the river." "See that you tell no one." "Tell the priest"). If we do not do what we have been prompted to do, whether due to neglect or not recognizing the voice of the Spirit, we may lose the blessing which we requested and was given. I learned a hard lesson about this, too.

I received a prompting from the Spirit telling me that I would receive a blessing that would make my life considerably easier. While I did not receive any words telling me about the things that I would receive, I understood. I was told to "tell no one" about the blessing. Because it was early in my education, I did not recognize the Spirit's voice clearly enough and so I told my daughter that I thought I received a prompting, telling me that I would be okay. I did not detail what I thought I would receive, but because I was told to tell no one and I told my daughter, I did not receive the blessing that was promised to me if I would have obeyed. Instead, I received a whispered chastisement when I noticed that I did not receive the blessing.

God decides how, when, and what is required to receive his blessings. I do not understand why some tasks are required for some blessings and not for others, but I know that he knows. I also know that these hard lessons teach us more profoundly than anything else. All things that God requires are to strengthen your faith or to gain wisdom, so if he requires you to do something, it is for his purposes and for your good. He would not require anything arbitrarily.

How long will it be until I receive my answer?

How and when God blesses us is his choice to decide, not ours. Part of surrendering to God's will is accepting how and when he gives you blessings. There are times, for example, when God appears to delay blessings incrementally. Many such blessings are usually in response to asking for healings, but they are not only limited to them. Understand that this is by no means a negative response. The most powerful healing blessings are those that look and feel like a lever has been flipped, causing the illness or ailment to be pushed toward a healing path, rather than to continue down its current path toward further suffering and disease. This is not a lesser healing than an overnight or instantaneous healing; just a different one. If you think about it, rather than flipping the course from disease to healing is easier on the body and reduces a shock of the system. While God is able to heal the body without a shock, thinking this way helps us to accept the amazing miracles that they are. Of course, you may also experience instantaneous healing, usually overnight. I am grateful for all the healings that I have received.

My right shoulder was badly injured in an automobile accident. The insurance covered the recommended therapies but did not completely heal the injury. For two years the doctors recommended that I keep my shoulder very still and not use it. Of course, not using the right shoulder meant always lying on the left side at night, which in turn, stressed the left shoulder joint to the point where it caused me similar discomfort and pain. Since the recommendation of the therapy caused the injury to the left side and not the accident, the insurance would not cover therapy to the left shoulder. For a little over a year, I could not use either arm except from the elbows down. So, I asked very specifically (or so I thought) for God to heal both shoulders, so I have full range of motion. I received a nudge in that direction and within two months, I had full range of motion, but the searing nerve pain continued and did not go away for several more months. So, I went back to God and asked for the nerves in my shoulders, arms, neck, and any other areas affected, to be healed so that I was not in any more pain, explaining that I was not sure exactly what caused the pain. Nearly overnight, I had a great reduction in my nerve and arm pain, but I also received some tests to my faith. When I felt the twinges of nerve pain, I simply acknowledged that I knew that Jesus is still able, and the twinges left until the next tests.

God chooses how and when he answers our requested blessings. That is part of his will. Watching for how God answers you, helps you to learn his will. Try to think about it this way so that you see it as a good thing, rather than a frustration.

Most of the answers to my requests, however, occur overnight. Understanding that God never causes confusion or delays answers to prayers, most of his answers would be given relatively quickly. We also see in the story of Abraham's servant that he was surprised by the quickness of the answer. He received it just as he finished his prayer. I have received answers immediately, within two minutes, overnight, and there is a couple of things that I have yet to receive. The answers to requests that have yet to be answered are things that he shows me are coming. He shows me that he is bringing all of the *players* into position so that he can give me the blessing when the time is perfect. But like I said, most of my requests happen overnight.

What do I do when nothing happens?

(Review the chapter, 'Ask and Ye Shall Receive') God is a being of order and perfection. This means that he cannot cause confusion and we need to learn to do things his way. So, what happens when nothing happens? As perfect Gods dealing with imperfect beings, we know that if there is an error, it is ours.

God does not let us sit and wonder. That would cause confusion. If your request aligns with God's will and you have asked in a way that he can answer, he will give you your request. It is that simple. It is promised in the Bible (ask and ye shall receive). Other than asking for an evil request, the only ways that God cannot or will not answer are if:

1. Your request takes your or someone else's agency;
2. You have not been specific enough so that he can give you your request;
3. You have forgotten to acknowledge your belief that God/Jesus is able, at whatever level you honestly believe;
4. You have a conflict in you that causes double-mindedness or otherwise ask something that is amiss;
5. You have unrepented sin that separates you from God;
6. You have not engaged your heart; or
7. You do not recognize the answer.

God would let you know by either giving you your request, or telling you that the answer is "No" in some way (by a stupor, chastisement, or other way). Because delaying the answer would cause confusion, you will receive the answer promptly, usually within twenty-four hours or overnight. There are some requests that require God to orchestrate all that is necessary to bring you your request. These requests take time to bring together; but even these answers are not "No" answers.

When I received Job's name in my mind and the flood of emotion, that morning, letting me know that I had gone through my test of my resolve as Job did, and telling me that it was over, I asked that he bless me as Job had. I knew that I had lost everything, lost most of the people I loved, lost my reputation, and so many other things. I asked God that he bless me as Job did. While it has been about eight years since I received this message, I have not yet received my request. There are times, however, when my Savior shows me or prompts me to know that it is not quite time yet. Other people's agencies are considered, even with these requests. I can feel that I will receive my blessing at sometime, in his own perfect way, when he has it ready for me.

Since I understand tests of faith, we must also understand that it is always *darkest before the dawn*. This also happens in our faith. Especially when we have learned and have grown in our faith, we can receive difficult tests of our faith right before the blessing is given. This is when we need to hold our faith, never wavering, not allowing it to shake and crumble, until we receive the blessing for which we have asked.

Agency for someone else: Look at the way that you word your request. Does your request take anyone else's choice? You may believe that you know what is best for another person, and you may actually know what is best for them, in that instance, but you cannot ask God for something that goes against that person's agency. This is one of the things that we *ought not* request. God will not answer any request that goes against someone's agency, for any reason. So, look at the wording of your request (since your words show your agency). Write it down so that you can see what you are requesting. Look for words that require the other person to do anything, and then change the words.

Most of the time, we ask God to do something for another person that would make them happy. First, happiness is a choice that the other person may not want¾there are some people who feel more comfortable when they are miserable. They have the choice. Second, you may have requested that God bless that other person so that they learn or see something. While you can ask for God to show another person something, you cannot ask to help them to see it. There is a difference. To show someone something is like turning on the television, for example, while they are in the room; where to help them to see it is more like forcing them to look at it, examine it, and perhaps consider it. We can ask for God to show them something, but not help them to see.

Finesse is needed to word a prayer for someone else so that it does not go against their agency. To make it easy, remove all requests for the other person to do anything. Separate your will from the other person's will just like you separated your will from God's will. Write down your request, looking at it closely and remove all words that request *any* requirement or action from the other person. You may ask God to find something that is best for that person, help them find something that they can live with, find something that will make them happy in their own way, etc. It is a good idea to add words that allow their agency to be their own. To pray that your son find a big love, for example, add "regardless whether he chooses to marry or not" or "one that helps him find satisfaction and happiness in his own way." That allows and protects his agency. Adding wording that allows the other person's choice may make all the difference in your prayer.

Agency for self: Because doing something may go against your own agency, in your prayer, change more general words (asking for help, asking for a healing) to ones that are more specific (heal my sight, make me walk, heal my feet to be like they were when I was a child, etc.). God cannot answer general prayers because of your agency, not knowing exactly what we are asking for, in our request, and may cause questions about whether it was actually God blessing you, or just happenstance. When you request very specifically, we know that it was God blessing you because it was given in exactly that way, therefore strengthening your faith.

Double-mindedness: Most double-mindedness comes from a conflict between your words and your emotions. Emotions, even those that you are not aware of, can cause double-mindedness. While your words ask for a blessing from heaven, your emotions can undermine them because God hears our hearts' greatest desires, even the desires that we cannot request, saying that you are not worthy or other fears.

Look at what you are feeling, as you request anything from God. Are you feeling anxiety or fear about asking for your desire? Are you nervous about asking God because you do not know if he will give you what you want or need? Are you worried about being worthy for the blessing? Are you afraid what will happen if you do not receive the blessing? Stuffing your emotions will not work. God will see them anyway. Isolate and identify your feelings before you take your request to God. Identifying your double-mindedness is part of constructing an effectual prayer.

Look for other types of double-mindedness. In the chapter, 'Ask and Ye Shall Receive,' we learned about the types of double-mindedness. Understanding that any type of conflict between the words you use to request a blessing and any other part of you (emotions; actions; behaviors; beliefs; attitudes; any hypocrisy, like being a Sabbath Christian; etc.) is double-mindedness, and you are required to rectify the conflict in order for God to be able to bless you.

The easiest way to rectify any double-mindedness that is not behavior-/action-related is to acknowledge everything that causes it and ask God to accept your words rather than anything that you feel, with your agency. Using your agency to ask God to highlight your words and disregard your emotions, and anything else that causes a conflict, is an excellent way to do this. If your double-mindedness comes from behaviors, attitudes, or actions, however, you will need to change it because behaviors, attitudes, or actions illustrate your agency.

Unrepented Sin: God cannot bless you while you are guilty of unrepented sins because you have distanced yourself from him. Take a moment and repent now. It does not take but a moment to repent, for the most part. If you are concerned that you may have some forgotten sins, ask forgiveness for those, too, asking for God to remind you of sins of which you need to repent, so that you can repent appropriately. To repent, you need to engage your heart and feel sorry for the sins that you have committed. This may be difficult to do if you do not know what you have done; but thinking about all of your sins (or the ability to sin at all) may help you to remember forgotten sins and feel enough emotion to repent. Most likely, if you do not remember any unrepented sin, you may be okay, but even repenting for those that you may have forgotten, especially if you feel the heart-felt emotions necessary to truly repent, may be enough for God to forgive you.

Remember that because God cannot give you any of his Spirit while guilty of sin, if you feel his Spirit, you are free of sin and are forgiven of all of them. This is how you can know where you stand with God. If you need to put yourself in a place that you usually feel God's Spirit, perhaps listening to a particular hymn, listening at a powerful sermon, being in the mountains, etc., and you do not feel the Spirit, you know that you need to repent for something. You may also ask for a *wisdom stupor*, asking for God to give you his Spirit if God sees that you are forgiven of all of your sins; or an *oblivion stupor*, asking that he remove the guilt, shame, anxiety, etc., that you are feeling if you have been forgiven from your sins, to show you that you have been forgiven. Feeling guilty for sins that God has long ago forgiven distances you from God and may be Satan tempting you.

You have done something wrong: Do not be afraid to talk to God about anything and everything. He loves you and is far more patient than you can imagine. Ask for guidance so that you can figure out what you have done wrong. Tell God that you know that he is perfect and so that the error is yours, and then ask him for your help to rectify it. Listen for a small prompting, and then follow it. Then, pray and make your request again. I hesitate to remind you that I did not have a book that told me how to rectify things. I relied on the Spirit to learn what I had done wrong. Listening to the small promptings to teach me (and the bugs—yuck!), I learned my way. You can learn your way, too, by listening for and following the promptings from the Spirit. He is your best teacher.

Do not be afraid to ask for blessings: It goes against our nature, as humans and Christians, to ask for blessings. Asking for blessings from God makes us feel all sorts of icky emotions. Feeling *un-humble*, selfish, and ungrateful is only the tip of the iceberg. We also experience a bit of rebellion when we do not ask, thinking that we should deal with it ourselves. But we do not see things as God does. Our Father in heaven knows that asking is the only way that we can really learn about him and his Son. God wants you to learn his ways, and wants you to be blessed, so ask. This is how we learn. Jesus completely relied on his Father, in his life, and we need to learn to rely on Jesus for all things. This is truly how we learn to "rest on the Lord." Remember, there are no limitations on blessings. There are no limitations on miracles.

Do I have to acknowledge that God is able every time?

The story of Jesus turning water to wine is such a fascinating story, for several reasons. This gives additional insight, between the lines, about the use of faith, and answers this question.

Jesus and Mary had a very close relationship. It was a relationship of a son and his mother. It is the type of relationship I have with one of my own sons. You can see the tenderness in this account. Yet, in all the records of Jesus and Mary, not once does it record anything about her acknowledging that she knew that Jesus was able. If it was important for us to acknowledge that she knew that Jesus was able, it would have been in there, right? It does not fit the pattern..., or does it?

Pondering the account and looking at my own experiences with my own son, I see that Mary would not need to acknowledge that Jesus was able every time. Mary knew who Jesus was before conception. Having an angel tell her that she will bear God's Son creates quite a belief. But Mary also watched Jesus throughout his childhood. If the Gnostic Gospels are correct, Jesus brought a bird to life that had fallen in a tree and died. Another Gnostic Gospel story tells about baby Jesus' bath water healing people. Regardless of whether these accounts were true, there would have been so many stories throughout his childhood that Mary would have seen firsthand.

Mary would not need to acknowledge that Jesus was able because she would have had a perfect knowledge. Likewise, there are no accounts about Mary and Martha, the sisters of Lazarus, acknowledging their belief that Jesus was able. While the New Testament does not explain their relationship to Jesus, it is obvious that they had known him for a very long time; perhaps, all of his life. As close as Lazarus, Mary, and Martha were to Jesus, I am sure that they had a perfect faith in him, too.

Once you have grown in your faith, so that there is no doubt, and you have grown confident in your faith, you will not have to acknowledge your belief that Jesus is able each time, too. You will only need to acknowledge when there is an imperfect faith. I think of the account of the woman who had hemorrhaged for twelve years. Perhaps she may have had a perfect faith. She was confident that if she would brush the hem of Jesus' garment, she would be healed. Certainly, he felt her faith before he saw her.

I do not believe that I have a perfect faith, even after all that I have experienced in the past eight years. As I grow, however, with each experience, I get closer. That is the reason we should ask for a lot of blessings from God, so that we may gain those experiences that perfect our faith. There are some requests that I may simply ask and I know that it will be done. Most of these types of requests are those that are similar to other requests, in different circumstances; or requests about which I have received promptings or messages regarding them, and so I know that God will do them for me. That means that I am becoming more confident in my faith. Perhaps this is showing me that my faith is being perfected. Then, there are times when I acknowledge my belief that God is able. I sense the difference somehow. There are times when I feel the need to explain my belief and I feel that I need to acknowledge it. I acknowledge most of the time as a sense of humility, knowing my place, as I converse with God. You will find that, too, as you continue using your faith to create that relationship. If nothing happens, then it is a good time to try again, acknowledging your belief that God is able. I am sure that God understands your belief and faith far more than you do. It would be better to error on the side of over-acknowledging, rather than to not receive the requested blessing because you did not think you needed to.

What do I do if I begin to doubt?

Many may think that the surprising awe that we experience, after a blessing is received, is doubt. Awe (the surprising feeling that questions, "did this really happen?") is what we feel toward God when we experience his mercies. Wondering is part of the human frailties that still does not completely comprehend God. We can wonder and still have faith, however. Faith is the acceptance and understanding that God is able. We can still wonder if the blessing is *working* or if God has answered our prayers, and still understand and accept that God is able. So wondering can still allow faith (meaning that *this* is not doubt). We do not know that we have actually received a blessing until we recognize it, which may require sight or sensation. Remember that Thomas, one of Jesus' apostles, still had faith in Jesus even though he had to wait to see the resurrected Christ before he would believe that he was really alive again. It is simply that he had not advanced in his faith to that point yet. Others ran to see if he was really there, too (you can see that I view Thomas differently, seeing his human imperfections rather than his doubt). Doubt is a belief that Jesus is not able, but Thomas believed in Jesus. Thomas simply may have not understood about *that* part of Jesus' abilities—not advancing enough in his faith to understand completely that Jesus truly was able to do ALL things—even rise after being dead for three days. I am sure that he believed that Jesus was able once he saw that he was no longer dead. When we wonder and then see that the blessing has been given, we are grateful and our faith is stronger than before. Eventually, your faith will be strong enough to believe, even without seeing. We have to learn by steps. Doubt can never solidify our faith, where awe and wonder can.

Doubt is an *uncertainty, unsureness, indecision, hesitation, dubiousness, suspicion,* or *confusion.* As you can see from this list, we do not doubt when we feel gratitude and awe. Instead, it is our human side trying to explain something that we have not experienced before. Doubt is more about double-mindedness than wondering. In fact, feeling nervous about requesting a blessing is not doubt if you go through it and ask. However, if you hesitate, then you are experiencing doubt. If you hesitate in following through the prompting, you are experiencing doubt. Yet, this is all part of the learning process. Repent. Acknowledge that you experienced doubt, and try again. The Father will forgive you and will give you another try.

In Mark (Mark 11:23-24), Jesus said that doubt occurs in the heart. This also means that all of the wild thoughts that run through your mind, after you have requested a blessing from God, is not doubt. It can cause some doubt, however, if you do not control your thoughts and buy into what they say. Doubt questions whether God is actually able. Saying aloud that you know that God is able helps to quiet some of the doubts that may come about. Separating thoughts from emotion, for doubt is an emotion, brings you back to the question that Jesus asked of all people whom he healed: Do you believe that I am able to do this thing? Focusing on what you truly believe about Jesus' ability helps you to get through any doubt. Our thoughts can cause you to doubt, but most of these thoughts come from the tests of your faith, testing you to see if your faith is truly unwavering or unshakable. You need to recognize these times, knowing what you need to do to pass the tests.

What if you fail a test of your faith?

Failure is not really failure if you learn from something that was not successful. Learning from failure is part of developing life-changing faith. I find that when we have been shaken from tests of our faith, for instance, they are not as much failures as frailties. Infants learn to walk by falling down, picking themselves up, and trying again. We will fall. Part of discipline is failing, trying again, and learning not to fail at some point in the future. Remember that God never required us to be perfect, in this life. From learning, growing, failing, and trying again, we can be perfected. We learn from our frailties. We learn deep and unforgettable lessons from failing, too. With God, there are no failures as long as you continue trying.

If you find your faith is shaken, acknowledge that you began to doubt, and re-acknowledge your firm and unwavering belief again, asking for God's help in keeping your faith unshakable ("Help thou my unbelief"). If it helps, add that you choose to continue to believe, using your agency—even if you do not completely believe it yourself (sometimes we have to talk ourselves into believing). Just make sure that you acknowledge it all to God. Trying to hide anything from him will never help you.

I failed many lessons and tests of my faith, but it helped me grow in my confidence with God. Failing taught me just as much, if not more, than my successes. Only after I messed things all up did I deeply learned the important lessons. Of course, I was given the test again, at another time, and I knew how to pass the test. Failing give me a whole and rounded understanding, which I would not have received if I only succeeded at every test.

There was a time recently when I had a large bout of doubt. It was regarding bed bugs again. Fears give us a great deal with which we may grow and learn. Being a resident manager at an apartment complex, I was told about which apartments had bed bugs, so that I did not enter their apartment (to change a light bulb, reset a thermostat, change a battery, etc.). I was standing very near the exterior doors of the building, talking to another resident who had a possible emergency and was trying to ascertain if it was an actual emergency or something that the property manager needed to deal with, the next day. There was a resident who was annoyed by the partial blocking of the door, as she took her dog outside. Rather than waiting for a minute or even excusing herself, she pushed her way through, allowing her dog to brush against my side. I would not have thought too much about it but her apartment was one in which had a large infestation of bed bugs, and had for some time because she refused treatments. Because of my strong fear of beetles, I panicked. I did not handle things well.

That night, I could not sleep. I felt critters crawling all over me, as my nervous system went into overdrive. I had asked for God to protect my apartment of beetles and even received several confirmations that he was protecting me, but I was too afraid. It did not matter how many times I said to myself that "I trusted Jesus," I could not get through it. For several days and nights, I felt bugs crawling on me.

About one a.m., I was struggling with the Spirit. I did trust Jesus! I know that he is able! Why could I not get through this?! Finally, I prayed. As I told God all that I was thinking and feeling, I received a prompting. It was the words said by the man who brought his son to Jesus to be healed, and said: "Help thou my unbelief." What a curious thought. I wondered.... So, I asked my Father to "Help thou my unbelief." What happened after was unexpected and amazing.

I learned that this is not a plea. It is a tool that we can use. "Help thou my unbelief" is a request for a healing on our faith. Within seconds, my nervous system calmed, my faith strengthened, I fell asleep, and I have not had fear about bed bugs since. I have had tests of my faith, however, many times since then, trying my faith so that I trust and know that Jesus is able and is willing to bless me, but I easily passed those tests (Yeah!). I was healed on my faith.

At some point, you may come across a doubt that you cannot get through, like my doubt that day. The Spirit is an excellent teacher and one that is constant—he will teach you throughout your entire lives, if you want to. I learned that day that, like a stupor, you may request to ask God to "Help thou my unbelief" and he will give it, as a healing blessing of your faith. God is so good, so merciful, so patient, so amazing!

How will you know if you receive the blessing after the test of faith?

Simply, there is no need to test your faith unless God is going to grant your request for the blessing. What you need to focus on is passing the test.

How long can I expect to have my faith tested?

Since the testing of our faith helps to perfect it, which is what the Bible says must be done and what needs to happen before Christ's Second Coming, you will have your faith tested until your faith is perfect, like Jesus' faith. Since this will not happen in this life, the short answer is that you should expect tests of your faith throughout your life. Passing the tests of our faith only requires the re-acknowledgement of our faith that Jesus is able, at every level. It is not a hard test.

Our faith must be perfected and the only way to do so is to be tested. With each blessing asked and every test given, our faith grows firmer, more unwavering, and more unshakable in all areas, until we trust God completely, even when faced with something extremely scary. In that case, we are able to look at the situation, without fear, and know that God is in charge and all is well, no matter what. You may feel the alarm or shock, but you will feel the confidence and peace within you, no matter what is happening around you.

We need the power of our faith in this life, as well as through the Second Coming. We need the blessings that are received from heaven. Walking through this life, we will be bombarded with temptations, enticements, and evil forces, whether we know about them or not. We need the protections, guidances, and blessings from God and his Son. We will not have a firm, unwavering, unshakable faith as we face Jesus, in the Judgment, unless we have had our faith tested in this life. It does not simply appear. We have to build that type of relationship, "precept upon precept, precept upon precept; line upon line, line upon line; here a little, and there a little".

Developing life-changing faith is a lifelong pursuit. The tests of your faith can be viewed as a blessing or a curse. I usually look at the positive side of life rather than the negative side, so I look at the positive side of these tests. The tests of your faith do several amazing and wonderful things—blessings really. Tests to your faith help us to realize that our Father and our Savior are very lovingly mindful of us—is lovingly mindful of *you*. It also exercises your faith, works your spiritual muscles. It keeps our faith healthy and strong. You will learn to be grateful for the tests of your faith and all the information that God and our Savior send to you, after the tests. You become happier, more peaceful, and more confident, in all aspects of your life.

A better way to look at tests of our faith is that we receive frequent reminders that God is very aware of us, and is willing to bless us with all the things that we ask of him. That is an amazing understanding. Then, they ensure that we have the tools and information needed to be with them again. Building this type of relationship with God helps us to feel close enough to experience them (their love, power, mercy) in our everyday life. It puts us in a place to know that our life pleases God. If we are not pleasing God, it means that we are bound to unrepented sin. So, if we receive tests of our faith, not only will we receive the blessings which we request, but we know that we are also sinless, because the Spirit cannot answer us when we are still guilty with sin. What a great side effect of asking and receiving blessings, and tests of our faith.

Instead, after you have requested a blessing from God, open that channel toward the Spirit and look for tiny promptings. I have said it before; you do not want to miss tests of your faith simply by overlooking them. Tests of your faith are what help your faith grow. Expect them. Look for them. If you have *any* thought, whatsoever, that you may be being tested, acknowledge that God is able, right then. You do not want to miss the tests of your faith from your unknowingness.

What types of tests can I expect?

That is a difficult question. Since I only receive tests of faith that I need, and you may need different tests of your faith, we may or may not receive the same ones. Also, I had been given the tests of faith to correct my misconceptions and to teach me all I explained in this book. Because you have learned all of this in this book, you may not need these tests of your faith. As I was taught these concepts, each teaching had a test of faith associated with it, in order to receive the full understanding. That means that I received a new concept and a new test of my faith nearly every week, or so. You may not need to receive tests on these concepts since you have learned about them by reading and experimenting on them, fully understanding by reading, pondering, and trying what I have written.

Since I have only experienced my own education on faith, and have never experienced anyone else's, I do not know what tests you will receive. God ensures that your tests will be applicable to you, personally, regardless of whether you have the same ones that someone else has, or not. Know that they will not be difficult or painful. Listen to what you feel and think. Simply do what is required, and then you may learn the wisdom that comes after the test. You do not want to miss your tests. After the tests is when you receive the full understanding of the concept being taught. This is when your faith is expanded. This is when you truly learn about Jesus.

What happens beyond developing life-changing faith?

Once you have received your basic education about faith, which will consist of learning to do the things in this book, you will learn to have a fully developed life-changing faith. This is the understanding that you are able to create the life of your dreams (but this is for a different book). This will include the knowledge, trust, and confidence that God will do all things that are expedient in him. What this means is that if it will help his purposes, he will do it. You will understand and feel his hand in your life. What are God's purposes? His purpose is to build a people with strong faith in his Son so that they can return home to him and receive all that he has for them. Just like young David, we will develop a firm confidence to look at past blessings, see what God has done for us, and move forward with the knowledge to see what he is willing to do for us in the future. In fact, because God will not give to some of his children and not to others, all the blessings that we have heard or read about, in the Bible or anywhere else (including others' witnesses), are also available to all of us.

As you grow in your faith, the tests of your faith will change, as our Father will ask you to do things to make you be more like his Son. Your faith will be tried harder than in the beginning. You will be asked to sacrifice the things that keep you from more faith, more understanding, and more blessings. You will have thoughts in your mind that will teach you to become the kind of person that Jesus is, asking you to focus on treating people more like he did.

As you get to this point, you will not hear the promptings as *loudly* as you did in the beginning. The Spirit becomes silent, as he teaches you to *sense* promptings and *feel* the messages of the Spirit without the thoughts and apprehensions that you receive in the beginning, learning to more concisely find God's frequency and keep that channel open, like Abraham did.

Your teachings will change, too. This change may make you feel insecure. Your fears will be addressed, and you will need to use your faith in Jesus to address them. If you are like I was, that means that you fail almost constantly, struggling and fighting to gain any success. But by the end of this level, you will see that the failures, the struggling, *were* the successes because you kept moving forward, changing, and growing in your faith. You will be required to ask and use the various tools (like stupors) to gain the answers, rather than him giving them to you automatically, like he did early on in your education. Do not be afraid of this change. You will need to assess where you are in your journey. God will still work with you. I had to ask for stupors almost weekly to learn whether or not I was doing well, asking for the anxiety of not knowing to be removed if Jesus sees that I am doing well, in his eyes, because while I could see my successes in the beginning, I could not see them in this level. Of course, Satan wanted to make me feel badly about myself, during my obvious insecurities, trying to impede any more spiritual growth. Continuing to acknowledge that God is able, each time that anything happened, got me through it; even though I did not know until I cleared that level.

The tests of your faith will change too, in this level. While your tests of your faith will make sense to you in the beginning, it will not make any sense, at all, in this part of your journey. You may receive communications over and over again that you may not recognize, because of the silence (you are not warned that the Spirit becomes silent). Multiple messages/chastisements (occurrences) that you receive over and over again are communications from God. It is him guiding you closer to his frequency, and the reason why you may feel insecure as you learn what he is doing (see Genesis 41:32).

Just as I stepped into this new level, I had the flu, which I had not experienced for many years (I take olive leaf and oregano capsules daily to kill bacteria and virus that may get into my body without the resistance that antibiotics cause). Because I had stepped into this level of my faith, and the Spirit's voice was silenced, without warning, I had experienced back-to-back flu four times and was going into the fifth time when I figured out that God may be giving me a message. As I felt the flu symptoms begin, for the fifth time, I immediately started asking God what I had done wrong, thinking that this was a chastisement (or worse, something done in Moses' time, in the wilderness). I started begging God for forgiveness, thinking that I had done something that gave me this *plague*. As I begged God, he prompted me to do something. Even though it was in the middle of the night (2 a.m.), I immediately did it, and the flu immediately fizzled out and I did not have it again. After I did what I was prompted to do, I gained the understanding of this new level. This level was to struggle to find the Spirit's voice, in the silence: to find God's frequency. The requirement to *sacrifice* something, to throw it out, which required me to take it to the dumpster at 2 a.m. rather than simply throwing it out in my apartment's trash can, was the test to pass this level and move to the next level of my faith. Luckily, this level only lasted a couple of months and I was taken to an entire new journey on faith (I am writing this down in a new book).

No matter what God does in your life, it is always for your benefit, to expand and strengthen your faith in Jesus. As long as you continue working with him, never telling him to stop (which would use your agency), God will teach you, and you will benefit from it. Remember that each level of your faith takes you closer to Jesus, and allows your Father to change you to be more like his Son. We become God's children and we shed off the symptoms of our corruptible flesh. By doing this, we are greatly blessed because we continue to obey his commands and desire to continue learning from him.

As you grow developing life-changing faith, you come to the understanding that not only is God willing to bless your life generally, but that he will bless your life personally. Many times this understanding comes through being blessed time after time after time, like with my experiences. This understanding cannot be forced, but comes as you continue on your journey working on life-changing faith.

You will learn that you may turn to God about anything because everything that is important to you is also important to him, including things that you consider to be embarrassing or too personal. Nothing is too personal or too embarrassing to God. He made you. He knows you inside and out. You will feel empowered to open all parts of you to him, and talk to him about everything. The relationship will be that personal.

You will have inspirations that will encourage you to ask, so that you may receive. It feels like God is in the corner, raising his hand, excitedly saying, "Ooooh, ooooh, ooooh, pick me! I will do this for you!" I had such a blessing that ended being very significant to me, in my beliefs as a Christian, by one of these types of blessings.

I do a catering job for Christmas dinner, for a family when they come into Utah for the holiday. My late husband had been doing it for more than twenty-two years and when he passed, they asked me to continue doing it.

On Christmas day, several years ago, I had an emergency that I had to deal with. One of the tenants lit a candle and left her apartment. My daughter, who was helping prepare the meal, reported that a smoke alarm was beeping in an apartment. I found the tenant and we went to make sure that everything was alright. When I got there, there was a good sized fire on the ledge under the window. I ran to the extinguisher and put the fire out. The smoke alarm, in the building, was activated and we had to evacuate. The fire department came and two hours later we were able to go back in and continue to fix the meal. I had scheduled things with minute-by-minute precision, so losing two hours was a huge problem. I called my son and son-in-law to help cook. I threw together the pie crusts, for the pies (thank goodness, pies are my specialty), getting the guys to do just as much as they could. Then, it was time for the turkey to be put in the oven to brown. I took the lid off the electric roaster to find that it was nearly cold. I put the thermometer into the turkey and found that it was only 120 degrees Fahrenheit. The emergency had flipped the breaker so that I had no power to the turkey roaster for more than three hours. I started to panic. My daughter asked me what I was going to do. I put the oven on 450 degrees to do a fast brown and…. I knew what to do.

The story about Jesus turning water into wine came to my mind. I had 45 minutes before it was time to start the hour long drive to the house, for their Christmas dinner. I thought for a second and then told my daughter that "I am going to pray." I walked into my bedroom, closed the door, knelt down, and prayed.

> "Father, I need your help. I am thankful for your help, your guidance, to keep my mind clear as I dealt with the fire today. I am grateful for the protection that you gave us all, to keep me and my tenants safe. I am grateful for the ability to run fast enough to get the fire out quickly and without much damage to the building. Father, during the emergency today, the electricity on the roasting oven that was roasting the turkey for today's dinner was flipped and the turkey is only 120 degrees, not even close to being done. But I remember the story about Jesus' mother, Mary, who had a similar situation at a wedding party that she hosted, where she ran out of wine. Seeing her situation, Jesus told the servants to get some water from the well and he turned jugs of water into very fine wine for her. Father, I need help making this turkey cooked and be good for the family's holiday feast that I have been hired to do. I have done my best and have lost so much time over the fire. I know that you are able to cook this turkey because Jesus was able to turn the water into wine and I know you both are able to do all things. Likewise, I am pretty sure that you will do this for me because Jesus was willing to turn the water into wine for Mary. I am grateful for this knowledge and the faith that you have taught me to have. I love you so much and am so grateful for you and your Son. I ask in Jesus name for you to do this for me."

I walked back into the kitchen with tears in my eyes, put the browned turkey in the cold roaster oven, put foil over the top, and put on the roaster lid (I do not know why, I just did it). We put the food into the cold trunk of my car (it had snowed that morning), and drove the hour long drive up the canyon toward the family's home.

We packed in the food and explained what had happened, and what may have happened to the turkey. The woman who hired me said, "Well, let's see how it is." I sliced the center of the turkey, down the breastbone, to find that it was perfectly cooked and juicy. The family said that it was the best meal that they ever had!

There is no scientific way for a 120-degree turkey to continue cooking to perfection, in a cold roaster pan, put in a cold trunk, in a cold car, for an hour drive up a mountain in the snow. No physics can ever explain how it could end up being perfect, juicy, and the best the family had ever had¾a simile of Jesus turning water to very fine wine.

I told friends, family, and my own children of this occurrence, and they have told the story to friends and family to roll their eyes and not see the miracle before them. In fact, I have been nicknamed *the Turkey Lady*. Miracles should be large and significant events, right? Certainly, nothing as silly as a cooked turkey, in a cold roaster pan, in a cold car trunk, in the end of December, in northern Utah after it had snowed! Healings yes, but not a cooked turkey.

This was important to me. I needed to prove to myself that I could do it, since this was the first time I had fixed the meal since my late husband had died. Being a bit of a perfectionist, I wanted the family to enjoy it and their holiday feast. It was important to me, and I had a very good example in the Bible to show me that I could receive that kind of miracle. Making water into fine wine for a wedding party is in the same category of miracles, and so it was available to me. Plus, it proved a very significant lesson for my faith and my understanding, which meant that it was expedient. It made me feel closer to my Father in heaven and Savior. It made me feel more confident asking for blessings from him, which further strengthened my faith. Yes, it was expedient.

Even further through your journey of developing life-changing faith, you will start to understand that there are categories of blessings that you may request and receive, and you may request all within those categories. Recently, I had a test of my faith. There was the familiar wondering sensation with the thought *Category,* with the feelings that he had helped me many times with needed money, with my car, and so many other things, but the thought *Category* sat in my mind and heart. The understanding that came in the days that followed was that God was willing to bless me with all of the things that are in those categories—protections, healings, money, emotions/feelings, household (animals, help [servants], food [crops], like Job). Because this is a relatively new understanding, I cannot create a list of all the categories because I have not identified them yet. That is something for me, and you, too, to watch for and figure out; but I am looking for the remaining categories of blessings that are available from God.

Everything in the Categories are available to us. All healings are available to us. All help is available to us (for our jobs, cars, animals, children, food, etc.). All protections are available to us. All help in all categories illustrated in the Bible are available to us. Because God is not a respecter of persons, this means that he is not partial in any way, and all blessings in all of these categories (and those that we have not identified yet) are available to each one of us. The God of the universe is able and willing to help you to know that you are able to do anything that is put in front of you.

At this point, your journey may or may not be similar to my own. That is for you to find. Your Savior will guide you as you continue in your journey developing life-changing faith. The Spirit will lead you as you learn, develop, experience, and gain great faith and understanding. Passages and stories will be highlighted in your mind and in your understanding, as you read in your Bible, and you will learn how these stories pertain to your own life. You will gain insights from random things that will give you additional understandings. You will continue to experience daily blessings, protections, and miracles from God.

You may find those who may think that you are crazy, like those who call me the *Turkey Lady*, but you will not be able to deny the power in simplicity and see the miraculous in the seemingly mundane. Daily miracles will become treasures in your heart and in your mind, and you will smile as others see your pearls as simple pebbles, but it will be beautiful and powerful in your mind and your heart.

MY TESTIMONY AND WITNESS

The woman who had hemorrhaged for twelve years was the story that most often spoke to me. It was this story that brought me to my first healing and began my journey to understanding and developing life-changing faith. This beautiful story spoke to me because I am the type of person who takes risks and goes after what I want. This woman took matters into her own hands, devised a plan, and patiently waited for Jesus to pass by, knowing with all her heart that if she could simply get even the fringe of the hem of his garment to brush her hand, the power within the Christ would heal her of her twelve-year affliction.

In a doorway, in her weakened condition, this woman waited for Jesus to pass by before she reached a feeble hand out toward his sandaled feet. But then Jesus did something surprising and remarkable. Regardless of the crowd of people who were pushing, shoving, and pressing against him, for there were mobs of people trying to get his attention, Jesus noticed that out of all the hundreds of people in the square, there was one lone woman who had touched him in faith and with purpose, the purpose of being healed by him. He was startled and he stopped in his tracks.

He told one of his disciples that someone had touched his clothes. He said that virtue (power) had been taken from him—not that he lost power but that someone had plugged into his power. When he looked around and moved the people pressing behind him, he noticed this frail woman crouching down at the side of the road, probably very fearful, at that point, since she had been discovered. I would imagine that she immediately apologized in a panicked stutter, bowing herself lower to the ground, backing further inside the doorway to hide herself, as many of us would do in that situation. And then Jesus would have done what he always did. He would have taken her by the hand and lifted her to her feet, steadying her in her weakened condition, calmed the fear in her heart with his piercing eyes, held her in his strong and tender arms, and warmly told her that it was her faith that made her whole.

Tears would have welled up in her eyes (as they are in mine as I visualize this scene), as she felt the most exquisite and overpowering love she had ever felt. Even though there were hundreds of people packed in the street, in her heart and in Jesus' heart, too, at that moment, they were the only two people on the planet.

Jesus took notice that someone with faith in him had plugged into his power to be healed. This makes two powerful points. (1) It is our faith that produces the link to the Savior's power, not our deservedness (I worded this intentionally), and (2) Jesus takes notice when we plug into his power, through our faith¾and if you have tears in your eyes and a swelling in your heart, you have just plugged into his power and he notices you, right now, too.

Faith is a byproduct of righteous living. Blessings and miracles occur when people put forth faith in the Savior (an act of will—this is why the acknowledgment of our belief that God is able activates our faith). The desire to further please God is a natural consequence of the receipt of blessings from him. It is a glorious cycle and one that was created intentionally by God, at the beginning of time. Due to our agency, we must activate our faith and acknowledge our beliefs for God to give us blessings, because otherwise it would go against our agency.

The beautiful relationship that you can have, by developing life-changing faith, is far beyond what I can explain in words. You are sustained through each moment of your life and you feel it from them. You feel a continuous and powerful love, gratitude, and worship in your heart that actively burns—a prayer in your heart and mind or at least a prayer-like connection to God—a willingness to help when and where you are able, and the listening ear to and for those whispers that catch your attention (although just barely) that tell you things in your mind (thoughts) and heart (emotions) that the Spirit has for you. Worship ceases to be a weekly, only in church, occurrence to a continuous worship of our God and our Savior.

I testify to you in the name of our Savior, Master, and King, Jesus Christ, that the things that I have written on these pages are true and come from my own experiences developing life-changing faith, and are supported in the pages of the Holy Bible. I have tested them out and found them to be flawless, perfect, and with the principles that Jesus taught during his life on Earth. I have experienced many miracles in the past eight years, a life time's worth of miracles that continue today. I say this not to brag or bring about anything to me personally, but as a testimony of the infinite goodness and mercy of our Father in heaven and our Savior, to glorify them, and because of my great love and gratitude to them for all with which they have blessed me. God has shown me that he loves to bless our lives, and loves us to show forth faith sufficient for all sorts of miracles.

I have not seen mountains move but I have experienced many healings of my body, have received miracles of a temporal nature, and have seen many other miracles and healings for other people because of this understanding. I have had miracles happen on behalf of my son, my daughter, and my granddaughter, where the things which I have asked occurred in that same day, others received the next day, and yet others which I know they will receive at some future date. I have seen hearts change toward me from those of persecution to those of repentance, gratitude, and love. I have had protections from the Spirit that surpassed anything I can explain in words; even my life has been protected several times. Yet, most importantly to me, I have felt the fantastic and wonderfully humbling experiences (including chastisements) of the tremendous love of our Father and Savior for me and I know that I am important to them; and I know you can experience it, too. I know without doubt that God is able to do all things and because of that knowledge, I know that I am able to do all things that are expedient through the power of Jesus Christ and the faith that I hold. I tell you these things so that you know that you may receive of them, too, in your own life. I am nobody special. I am just like you. God has not blessed me inequitably. You can experience these things in your own life, too.

Now it is your turn to take this tremendous and blessed journey to developing life-changing faith. Please do not take my words only. I am a fallible human. Turn to the Bible. Turn to our Father in heaven in prayer. I have written this book constantly praying that our Savior's desires would be met here and that the words which he would have me write would be written, to glorify our Father in heaven and Jesus. It is for you that I have written these things, my brothers and sisters in the Gospel. Search the Bible to see if those things I have written here are true. Then, test them out. Knowledge is only gained after the faith has been proven and tested, and faith is tested only after its use.

Continue the development of your faith, always building on your knowledge and understanding, remaining close to your Savior in prayer, continually submitting your will to the Father's will and trusting in his wisdom. May God be with you always through your quests developing life-changing faith. May you find the mysteries of God that you have always desired. This is my prayer for you.

I leave my witness, in Jesus' sacred name.

Carole Haygood

I would love to hear from your experiences developing life-changing faith at my Facebook page: @DevelopingLifeChangingFaith

"If thou canst believe in him, all things are possible."
(Mark 9:23 KJV)

Printed in the United States
By Bookmasters